T

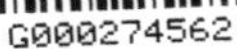

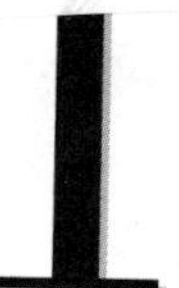

TITANIA'S NUMBER 1

Titania Hardie

For Nick

A CONNECTIONS EDITION
This edition published in Great Britain in 2007 by
Connections Book Publishing Limited
St Chad's House, 148 King's Cross Road, London WC1X 9DH
www.connections-publishing.com

British Library Cataloguing-in-Publication data available on request.

ISBN 978-1-85906-223-4

1 3 5 7 9 10 8 6 4 2

Phototypeset in Bliss and Natural Script using QuarkXPress on Apple Macintosh
Printed in China

Contents

STARTING THE JOURNEY

This little book of numerology invites you to be amazed by what you will learn from numbers – about your character, your tastes, your instincts, your relationships, and even about your future. But to do this involves a willingness to believe – as Pythagoras, the 'Father of Numbers' did – that numbers can provide a clue, or formula, through which we can perceive some of the evolving patterns and cycles that affect our own individual existence.

Let's find out more ...

Discovering numerology

Fans of Sudoku will understand how it entices us intellectually to see how strands of numbers – almost magically – slot together and interconnect with one another, revealing a rhythm of harmonious relationships between the lines. In one sense, numerology does this for us on a personal and spiritual level. The Science of Numbers, as it is called, suggests that there is an order and a rhythm in the universe of which we are a part, and although there is a certain mystery in the way numbers seem to function as symbols for our experiences, there is a long tradition across many cultures of their fascination for us.

Now, in an age of gigabytes, PINs and mathematic-based technology, how can we doubt the role that numbers play, or the way in which they have become part of our daily landscape? Numbers speak to us every day about our personal identity on this planet. Our birth date is absorbed by society as proof of our existence: you need it to be 'real' at the bank, in the office, when you travel, in an automated phone queue – in *all* official records. Indeed, many people consider the day-date of their birthday to be their lucky number. But can it really say anything about us?

Did you know, for instance, that:

- If you were a **5** or a **9**, you'd need to invest in good-quality luggage because you'd be bound to notch up a lot of air miles?
- Or that a **6** feels compelled to generously host open-house for guests and family?
- A **7** will want to specialize in whatever interests them?
- And an **8** would rather have one small quality gift than half a dozen less luxurious presents?
- Or that any friend who's a **4** will painstakingly spend

hours getting something just right, whereas a **3** will have several projects on the go at one time and get through as best they can? C'est la vie!

But you've picked *this* little volume because you're a **1**, which means you should always try to maintain significant personal freedom in your life and career, and even work for yourself if possible ... whereas if you had been a **2**, a partnership would be far better suited to your personality.

About this book

Each individual title in this series investigates, in depth, the meaning of one of nine personal numbers. *This* volume is dedicated to the exploration of the number **1**.

We will be focusing principally on your **DAY** number – that is, the number relating to the day of the month on which you were born (in your case, the 1st, 10th, 19th or

28th of the month). Calculating your **DAY** number is easy: you simply add the digits of your day together (where applicable), and keep adding them until they reduce to a single number (*see calculation examples on page 270*). And that's it. It doesn't matter which month or year you were born in – you just need the day-date to discover your **DAY** number. And *you're* a **1.**

Your **DAY** number reveals all kinds of information, and, working from this number, we will be considering:

- The obvious attributes of your number as they impact on your personality
- How you are likely to dress, and what colours or styles appeal
- How you react to things psychologically, and what drives or motivates you
- In which fields you will have the most natural abilities and gifts

- What annoys you most
- What sort of lover you are, and how you relate to all other numbers
- What the future holds

... and much, much more.

And you have another significant number too: your **LIFE** number. This is derived from adding up the digits in the *whole* of your birth date – day, month and year (*see examples on page 270*). What does *this* number mean, and what do your **DAY** and **LIFE** numbers mean in tandem? And how does it affect you if you're also a 'master' number (**11** or **22**)? Read on and you'll see. But first, let's meet your **DAY** number ...

So, you're a 1

The number **1** is **dynamic** and **self-reliant**, and belongs to the leaders and explorers of this world. Fear hardly gets a look-in: your number is a byword for **courage** and **independence**. A true individual, you are assertive – and, perhaps, even aggressive, if you feel that you're not being listened to. If you also happen to have a large number of 'A's or 'S's in your name (both of which have a numerical value of **1** – more about which shortly), you will exhibit especially strong qualities of independence and a fiercely **strong will**, preferring to do things entirely your own way. All **1**s strive to make their own discoveries and mistakes, rather than learning from anyone else's.

1 is strongly concerned with **action** and **energy**; every

1 gets bored easily, chafes under restraint, and absolutely hates to be inactive. Indeed, you are drawn to bold colours like flame red and apricot – your true colours – that help you to express the immense energy that comes with your number.

Those born under this number have a natural instinct about what is going on around them – a powerful sense of **intuition** that, rather than being something mystical, is more a **practical**, intelligent, discerning kind of knowledge that you possess. There is no shaking a **1**'s opinion once it is formed. Your **certainty** is always clear, and occasionally this means you have to bluff your way through obstacles you hadn't counted on finding. As a **1**, however, you never lack the **bravery** to tough things out, and you are quite prepared to stand alone when need dictates. In fact, if you take on the world and are at odds with popular opinion, so much the better. **1**s love to **lead by example** and blazon their way through uncharted territory.

You have excellent powers of **concentration** and **imagination**, but are no physical worker. You enjoy teasing out ideas and opportunities – especially in business – and will be known as someone who is a **decision-taker** with executive ability. For this reason, it's best for you to work in your own business if possible – **1**s need a lot of freedom – or, at the very least, independently within a larger organization.

Even when you do work for or with others, you are innovative and find your own techniques. And if you have an extra helping of the **1** characteristics, you will be **ahead of the crowd** and understand instinctively how trends are going to develop. You can sense what's going to be hot, and what's not, before anyone else even gets a whiff of it!

Number **1**s, at their best, are **inventive** and original, but this has negative propensities too. **1**s can be cynical and **contrary** towards others, and you must be honest enough to recognize that on your more ungenerous days – or when you feel thwarted by others who think more cautiously than you do – you can be **domineering** and **egotistical**. Remember that you are more likely to influence peers and loved ones if you are approachable, and that you sometimes have to slow down and be patient with those who don't see an end result as convincingly or clearly as you do.

Blessed with a **fine mind** and an excellent memory, **1**s are able to dwell on information and see the answer to what may be puzzling for others – thus you are the number that makes good professors or senior tutors, head teachers, managing directors and politicians. Distinctive dressers, and decidedly charismatic, **1**s are generally good public speakers, and rise to the task of addressing a group with **humour** and gusto. You exhibit **ingenuity** in your way of expressing ideas, and you may be **articulate** in a very clear way.

As long as you avoid being boastful, you will almost always impress those who look up to you, and will show them the way.

Sound familiar? Getting a taste for what your number is about? And this is just the beginning. You'll soon find out how the number 1 expresses itself as your Day number in each and every day of your life. But before we go any further, let's take a look at where all this first came from ...

What's in a number?

Numbers have always had a sacred meaning. The Egyptians used an alphabet that conflated letters and numbers, and, as such, each number exuded an idea that was more than the sum it stood for. There is a whole book of the Old Testament devoted to the subject; and the Hebrew language – exactly like the Egyptian – has a magical subtext of meaning where letters and numbers can be doubled to reveal an extra layer of secret, so-called 'occult' information. It is called the *gematria*, and forms a crucial part of the sacred occult wisdom called Kabbalah. There were twenty-two letters – a master number – in both the Greek (Phoenician) and Hebrew alphabets, and repetitions of the spiritual properties of the numbers **3** and, especially, **7** recur throughout the Bible.

The Father of Numbers

But modern numerology derives more formally from Pythagoras, the Father of Numbers, who was a serious and spiritual philosopher, as well as the man who explained some of the secrets of geometry. Born on the island of Samos, although he ultimately settled in Cretona, a Greek colony in southern Italy, he is understood to have travelled widely to both Egypt and Judea. Some accounts of his life also suggest he may have studied under the Persian sages of Zoroaster, but an analysis of his teachings certainly reveals the strong influence of Kabbalistic thought in his philosophy.

Pythagoras understood numbers as a *quality* of being, as well as a *quantity* of material value. In one sense, the numbers as figures were connected with the measuring of things, but 'number' itself was significantly different to this, and encompassed a spiritual value. The numbers from one through to nine represented universal principles through which everything evolves, symbolizing even the stages an idea passes through before it becomes a reality. Mathematics was the tool through which we could apprehend the Creation, the universe, and ourselves. Musical harmony was a sacred part of this knowledge, as was geometry, which revealed divine proportion.

Most importantly, Pythagoras believed that numbers were expressive of the principles of all real existence – that numbers themselves embodied the principles of our dawning awareness, our conjecture and growth. Through mathematics and number we could approach divine wisdom and the workings of the universe as a macrocosm. Thus, in microcosm, our personal 'mathematics' would unlock the workings of our own being, and help us to see a divine wisdom concerning ourselves. **1** was not just the first digit, but also had a character of beginning, of independence, of leadership, just as the number **2** was more than merely the second number quantifying two objects, but also implied the philosophical concept of a pair, of co-operation, of a relationship beyond the individual.

Pythagoras also believed that we could understand our direction and fate through an awareness of repeating cycles of number, making numerology a key to revealing our opportunities and our destiny.

By tradition, the doctrine Pythagoras taught to his students in the sixth century BCE was secret, and no one wrote down his ideas until his death. But Plato was a follower of Pythagoras and, along with the rebirth of Platonism, the ideas of the Father of Mathematics were revealed afresh during the revival of Greek learning in the Renaissance. The great magi of the fifteenth and sixteenth centuries explored anew the significance of number and the gematria, to understand the hidden messages of the ancients and of the divine mind. Mathematics as a philosophy was the bridge to higher realms of spirituality.

Essence of the numbers

one is the spark, the beginning, Alpha, the Ego of consciousness. It is male.

two is consort. Adding partnership, receptivity, it is female, bringing tact.

three is a synthesizing of both of these qualities and brings expansion and joy.

four is the number of the Earth, of the garden, and of stability. It brings order.

five is curiosity and experiment, freedom, changes. It brings sensuality.

six nurtures and cares for others. It will love and beautify, and brings counsel.

seven perfects and contemplates the Creation. It is intellect, stillness, spirit.

eight is the number of power, the octave, a higher incarnation. It brings judgement.

nine is humanity, selflessness, often impersonal and all-knowing. It brings compassion.

Applying the knowledge

A deeper understanding of the self can be achieved through an awareness of the mysticism of number within us; and both the birth date and, to some degree, our given name are the keys to unlocking our mystical, spiritual core of being. Exploring the affinity between letter and number can also reveal insights about the lessons we need to learn throughout our lives to improve and develop as individuals (*see page 25*).

This book looks at the significance of numbers as they affect us every day, focusing largely, as introduced earlier, on our **DAY** number. It is this number that reveals to us our instincts, our impulses, our natural tastes and undiluted responses, our talents and immediate inclinations. This is how people see us in daily situations, and how we behave by essence.

We will be exploring how our **DAY** number influences

our love relationships and friendships; at what it says about our career strengths and our childhood; at the way our number manifests in our leisure time; and at how it might give us a better understanding of what to expect in our future cycles, as we pass through any given year under the sway of a particular number. Each birthday initiates a new cycle, and each cycle seems uncannily connected with the philosophical concerns of the number which governs that year. Look both to the past and present to see how strongly the number-cycle can illuminate our experiences ... and then count ahead to ponder what may be in store over the next year or two.

And numbers also say something about where we live or work, about our car, and even about our pets. Understanding these secret qualities can add a new dimension of pleasure – not to mention surprise – to our journey through life.

A NUMBER TO GROW INTO

The presence of our **LIFE** number, however, takes longer for us to appreciate in ourselves – longer for us to grow into – and it often takes time to reveal itself. This number comes to the fore as your life progresses, and on pages 214–247 we will be looking at the meaning of your **DAY** number together with your individual **LIFE** number, to see what this reveals about your character and potentiality.

The **LIFE** number may intensify the experience of the **DAY** number – if it is closely related to it, or shares similar patterns. But more frequently our two different numbers clash a little, and this often allows insight into the aspects of our being where instinct pulls us in one direction but higher wisdom or experience mediates and pulls us in a second direction.

Who would have thought you could learn so much from a number? Pythagoras certainly did, over 2,500 years ago ... and now you will discover it too.

What's in a name?

Your name also has a story to tell, and it is a story revealed through number. Every letter corresponds to a number: in the Western alphabet we use twenty-six letters, which are at variance with the twenty-two formerly enshrined in the Hebrew and Greek alphabets. Some numerologists believe that this is in keeping with the more material world we now live in, as the number '26' reduces to '8' (when you add the digits), which is the number of power and money.

The correspondences between the numbers and the letters of the alphabet are as follows:

1	2	3	4	5	6	7	8	9
A	B	C	D	E	F	G	H	I
J	K	L	M	N	O	P	Q	R
S	T	U	V	W	X	Y	Z	

As you are a **1**, it is most revealing to look at the letters A, J and S, as they occur (or not!) in your name. This is because they intensify the experience and impression of your main number.

Indeed, to fully utilize all of the qualities inherent in your number, you should be using a name which is in poetic harmony with your **DAY** number. As a **1**, you will exude the courage and quickness you require to act upon your instincts and ambitions if you have a name which underlines these main **1** qualities. In other words, make sure you use a name which includes an A, J or S. This may sound strange, but many of us have our names shortened or completely changed by friends, family and lovers, so it is important to feel that our chosen name – the one that we use as we go about in the world – is making the best of our abilities and energies.

Among the letters that are equivalent to the number **1**, A is a vowel – and a common one, at that – so the chances are that you have a letter A in your name. It is very significant if your name begins with an A, for the vowels represent the soul in our name, and to begin a name with a vowel means the soul is very strong within the character. The first vowel in the name is also especially important, as this is where the soul is said to enter into our spirit – so if your first vowel is an A, you have an extra dose of the strength and independence associated with the number **1**.

The letter-numbers help us to act out our sense of purpose, and if these work in correspondence with the **DAY** number we are more likely to find our sense of will and achieve our goals more rapidly. But if we have few or none of the letters of our **DAY** number, we often feel it is much harder to shine in our field of opportunity. Let's take a closer look at what this means ...

Missing a '1' letter?

As a **1**, you will find you reach your career potential with greater ease if your business name includes one of the above letters. As a **1**, though, living up to your character traits can be demanding. Your number desires leadership and requires some private time and the room to experiment with unique pioneering ideas.

If your name lacks a '**1**' letter, you may feel that you are clear in your vision of what the world around you needs, or in what would make you fulfilled, but yet you struggle in finding the self-confidence that is normally so integral to a **1**'s character.

In your social life, your natural wish to try doing things your own way may be jeopardized if the name you use does not include one of these letters. Something as simple as varying the spelling of your name could change this, and mean that you learn how to assert your individuality and feel that you are being listened to. Get your peers and loved ones to give you a pet name to offset any imbalance.

Too many 'A's?

It can be just as much of a problem if your name carries a flood of letters which correspond to your number. This potentially gives you an overdose, and brings out some of the negative qualities associated with **1**.

A lot of 'A's in the name you use can make you too aggressive or headstrong, meaning that you fail to communicate with others clearly. You assume everyone is on your wavelength when they have no idea what you are talking about! Equally, a name with many 'S's can be either full of charm or scalding with sarcasm. Try to choose a name for everyday use which minimizes the number of '**1**' letters.

YOUR DAY NUMBER

It's a new day ...

You will learn a lot about the numbers of your birthday and your name as this book unfolds, but the DAY number is, to my mind, the most important – and sometimes least well-recognized – number of all ... the number which exerts a magnetic hold on us each and every day of our lives. Every time we react to a situation, an emotion, a provocation of any kind, we are shooting straight from the hip, as it were, and this reaction is coloured by our DAY number.

As we know, your 'Day Force', or **DAY**, number is **1** if you were born on the 1st, 10th, 19th or 28th of any month. Each of these different dates also affects us – the characteristics of the number derived from a birthday on the 10th vary intriguingly from one on the 28th, for instance – and we will look at these differences in the pages ahead.

All four dates, however, still reconcile to an overall **1**. This number determines your gut reactions and the way you express yourself when you are being most true to yourself. Your parents, lovers, friends and co-workers all know you best through this number.

So what is the theme of being a 1? What are you like when you're at work, rest and play? And how compatible are you with the other numbers? Let's find out . . .

1'S CHARACTER

Charms, graces, warts and all ...

For every single person born with a '1' birthday number, there is a little torrent of energy unleashed in the world! Yours is the number of action and intention, and it likes to get on with things from the first hour of its birth. With this DAY number you are an incident waiting to happen from the outset, and you have a complete intolerance for anyone who ever says the words 'I can't'. 1s don't understand this word, for they always find a way to do things. When there is no example to follow in history, you are the person who will create a new way of trying. You expect success, and you will find a means to that end in almost every case.

To boldly go ...

Your sense of daring astonishes everyone – even those who know you well. You never have to wait for a second invitation: if someone suggests something once, that's enough. You rush in where angels proverbially fear to tread, but you do this with such gusto and positivism that you are virtually certain to pull off the most difficult feats, your powerful memory often helping you to bluff your way through unknown circumstances.

Whenever you decide that you are unwilling to take no for an answer, you marshal all of your considerable gifts of charm and wit and manage to convince most people to see things your way, and to take a chance on what it is you're proposing. You are unlikely to quit until every possible avenue to propel you towards your goal has been exhausted. Nine times out of ten this will mean exploring new fields or creating fresh opportunities with the people around you, and nothing suits you better. Failure is not something you do!

You will find yourself volunteering to lead others through dark waters, but even if you hang back and say little you are still likely to be elected by others for what seem impossible tasks. You have the kind of synthesizing mind that sees numerous possible options inside the unlikeliest box of props, drawing on talents from a ring of friends or co-workers that they were unaware they had to offer in the first place.

This is part of what makes you a creator – someone who can virtually invent activities and projects for others to undertake. You see others better than they see themselves, and this bestows on you a natural executive status in business. You are able to see their potential, and you use your own energy to help them realize it, until everyone witnesses something completely new from the venture.

Keynotes of the 1 personality

Positive associations: energy, enthusiasm, bravery, quick wit, willpower, creativity, leadership skills, independence, self-motivation, inventiveness, charisma, pioneer mentality

Negative associations: aggressiveness, boastfulness, egotism, bossiness, domineering tendencies, impulsiveness, cynicism, narrow opinions, talking over others, ignoring others' views

For your career to extend you, and draw on all you have to offer, it must be varied, and you need scope to develop and explore new territories within any work field. Mundane work will confine you and blunt your sharpness, but you will flourish in any arena which demands that you use your initiative.

Action speaks louder than words

It's fair to say that you don't mean to exaggerate or boast sometimes about your exploits, but you may find a way to *remind* the slower and less active people around you that *you* have few difficulties in understanding complexities or launching yourself into the world. Idleness drives you mad, and so does hesitant thinking. You'd rather do the wrong thing – if so it proves – than sit on the fence. When you make mistakes, you are prepared to own up to them. This impulsiveness can mean that you wear a few scars, though, and it might be well to remember that the number **1** is related to the planet Mars, which governs scalds and cuts.

Whenever a friend or loved one lacks inspiration or direction, your company is the best remedy. You are the one who will bully, rather than cajole, them out of inertia, but you could become impatient and bossy with them if their state of impasse goes on too long. You have the knowledge of what must be in the world, and understand that there are no prizes for a failure to complete the course – but sometimes you will need to moderate the way you communicate this to others. Everyone who knows you well realizes that tea and sympathy is not offered at your table so much as a smack on the tail to get them moving again. Usually this works, and your bluntness is forgiven.

Your talent in life – across the board – is to visualize something new and get things moving around you, to make the new vision a reality. This will be true whether it relates to the home you live in, the work you do, the methods you employ to deal with others, or the way you want to orchestrate your lifestyle. You are always striving for something original, and your inclination will be to concentrate on an idea for a short time, work on the set-up stage to the point of near exhaustion, and then pass the blueprint on to some steady and reliable child-minder to actualize it. Your challenge – and joy – is in drafting the concept from scratch, but the 'hey-ho' solid grafting and routine work is not for you. Choosing a team around you who can accommodate this need is obviously crucial.

Going it alone

Relationships have an interesting dynamic for number **1**s. You love to be in the company of someone who surprises you, but you need to be with a very wise partner who knows exactly how to read what you don't say to them. Your number is often strangely reticent about its needs, partly because **1**s seem like such independent and self-regulating people that no one guesses how much, at times, they really do need others. You have only yourself to blame, in that you often fail to ask for help or lean on anyone's shoulder. You are used to going it alone, well rehearsed at being private and nursing grievances quietly, but this is frustrating for those who want to get close to you.

Of course, you also genuinely need time to be a loner, having the space to invent notions and compose ideas. If any relationship – business or personal – makes constant demands on your time or expects undiluted access to your leisure hours, it will cause problems for both parties.

Born independent

Events throughout your life have almost certainly conspired to make you think for yourself – from the earliest age. You have an array of talents and considerable personal stamina, and it seems the world often shapes the circumstances you find yourself in to make you draw on these qualities. As such, **1**s often miss out on having an easy childhood, and seem to be forced to find their strengths early on; but as you grow older, and discover your resilience and wit, you should find that life gets easier, and that you are properly allowed to be young at heart. This is often also true for those born with a **DAY** number of **5**, and yet they are not asked to be quite so independent and to stand alone, as you are. It would be true to say that the pattern of thinking deeply for yourself, of trusting your own counsel, and of learning to be authoritative, has been ingrained from the cradle.

Many people who know you only superficially will think you are aggressive and non-compliant, or that you seldom consult others' wishes as much as your own. There is some truth in this, for you often put yourself in positions of pressure, and pressure frequently brings out your aggression just to enable you to survive the intensity of what is expected of you. But aggressive behaviour is just as likely to be a defensive reflex, or an attempt to disguise the irritation you may sometimes feel at carrying the burdens for all those who depend on you. You are so used to friends and family leaning on you that you might be excused for having a short fuse at times. Also, you hate to be held up or made to wait, and impatience is definitely a problem for all those who share your **DAY** number.

When you feel under fire, or that you have to explain yourself, it would help to give yourself some breathing space, and take a long walk or engage in some other activity that uses up some of your energy in a more positive way than just exploding at the source of your frustrations.

Having a quick mind and an intelligent brain, you are critical of time-wasters and plodders, but also uniquely sensitive to criticism yourself. You will almost invariably find your own credo, with some highly unusual or independent beliefs that attract you. This means you find little sympathy for others whose minds are, in your view, fettered by traditionalism, but if your own sense of individuality is accentuated you may make even the people who are closest to you feel nervous and worried about you.

The main caution is to be aware that you do sometimes come across to others as excessively headstrong and

– more than just original – possibly even eccentric. This may be a huge point of attraction about you for some, but you may need to moderate your instincts in certain situations, whenever domineering actions threaten to be detrimental to your partner's or lover's feelings of self-worth around you. **1**s don't mean to be cruel, for they are not cruel: but they are sometimes unaware of others' sensitive corners, and of their lover's feeling of being unheeded – or even cancelled out.

Stand out from the crowd

The image you project to most people is of an independent and capable person who drives in the fast lane and gets – more or less – what they want. Others recognize your capacity to take control of a situation, and they know that you can run things smoothly. This makes you an automatic choice as class captain, local councillor, club chairperson, parent committee delegate or public speaker for a group. Everyone always expects you to get the job done, whatever job that may be. You are an ideas person – which all the world recognizes – and you have a clear idea of what it takes to sell your ideas to others, and begin marketing them. This means that you know how important image is, and that you will take some trouble to get it right.

You have a huge head start over many people because your personality is vibrant and forceful, and you like to dress with flair. Your personal style is distinctive, and the world sees you as a one-off. **1**s are trendsetters, but they are usually unconcerned about whether or not the passers-by observing them like what they see. Your number says, 'Take me or leave me,' and means it; you stand out from the crowd – and you like to. You prefer to bend the rules that exist or create a new set of options and, fashion-wise, you favour striking, original styles and designer labels. It's not money or power that you are trying to project, however: your concern is to avoid being a copy of anyone else. If someone has performed it, said it, or worn it before, you'll find something new to present. You can even be quite competitive in this regard. Bring on the exclusive designs and fresh seasonal colours!

It is your wont to unearth quiet little boutiques no one else has heard of, or to shop by internet so that your choices come from far and wide. Your sense of chic is usually sound – although it is not unknown for **1**s to be eccentric and loud in their fashion or colour choices, just to get attention. You will often push the boundaries of what many people consider to be 'in good taste'. Your number is nothing if not a breath of fresh air!

Forward thinking

Perhaps the most important advice for anyone with your number concerns the way you approach life. You already know that you are both strong-willed and experimental, but it is in your interest to continually seek fresh fields of self-expression. A **1 DAY** number shouldn't go backwards, but should be constantly edging forwards. If you don't feel you are achieving this, your sense of frustration and confinement will send you into a downward negative spiral. Remember: you are one of the progressive people in this world, and this does occasionally justify being stubborn or dictatorial. When your inspiration is high you are efficient and purposeful, and you need to trust that sense of purpose.

You love to win, and are used to coming out on top in most of the games you play. Nevertheless, you can become a higher-minded human being if you acknowledge that there are other people around you who have different needs, and that they will appreciate your attempts to include them in your thinking and your plans. No amount of praise for your excellent strengths and personal dynamism is an excuse for lapsing into total selfishness, or a justifiable reason for asserting your will at the expense of the right of those closest to you to personal expression. Wear your positive attributes with great pride, but try to minimize those stubborn character manifestations that can lead to sheer rudeness to others, or an impossible sense that you already know it all.

To conclude on an upward note, it is to your credit that experience will be a great teacher for you. You like to learn your own way, and nothing does this more than the passage of time and the crossing of many new frontiers again and again in your lifetime. You have such a propensity for mental energy and personal vigour, and such a capacity for quick understanding and focused thought, that you will almost certainly fit a great deal into your life, and rarely allow yourself to become bored or really negative for long. You are dissatisfied with the old ways of doing things, and this makes you a joy to have on board for almost any team, who look to your enthusiasm to get them off and running. True, you're usually more of an astonishing starter than a real finisher of what you start, but you are indeed a dreamer of wonderful dreams, and this means you have what it takes to show the rest of us the way forward.

1 in a nutshell

Personality watchwords: extrovert, individual
Lucky colours: scarlet, flame red, copper, apricot
Lucky herbs/flowers: basil, nasturtium, honeysuckle
Scents: cypress, coriander, pepper
Fashion style: modern, one-off pieces
Decorative style: modern, clean, strong colours
Letters: A, J or S (needed in the name you use)
Car style: fast, sporty, sunshine colours, or off-road vehicle
Holiday destination: off the beaten track!

Which 1 are you?

6 7 8 9 **1** 2 3 4 5

Everyone with a **DAY** number of **1** will exhibit many of the characteristics just discussed. It is interesting to see, though, how the number **1** varies across all of its incarnations. There is a subtle but definite difference between the way the number operates for someone born on the 1st of the month – which makes for a pure **1** effect – and someone born, say, on the 28th.

As a rule, anyone born on the single-digit date has the truest and most undiluted effect from the number, whereas someone born as a product of two digits borrows some qualities from the pairing of the numbers. Twenty-anything puts the softening digit '2' before the second number, and this usually means that, whatever number you are, you are more aware of the needs of others. Similarly, if '1' is the first digit (10th/19th) you are even more independent, and perhaps more assured of your self-worth than other **1** people.

Let's look at the variations across all the birthdays ...

Born on the 1st?

This birthday gives you all the **1** properties we've described in their clearest form. Original, self-willed, impulsive and charismatic, you are the most inspired starter – but you may lack the patience you sometimes need to finish a job. As an instinctive leader you will always prefer to leave the back-up tasks to others, and delegating is less a problem for you than for other **1**s.

Although you are private, reticent and rather undemonstrative emotionally, you still thrive on praise and encouragement. You are intellectual but not patient, and you need several areas of interest and many lines of pursuit on the go at the same time *just* to hold your attention. You may be the most independent and driven of all the **1**s, but you also need a lot of time alone. You often feel misunderstood by those who think you can stand by yourself, even though they should know you better and realize you are just unaccustomed to making emotional pleas. This doesn't alter the fact that you are a great survivor, but if you can develop your ability to ask for assistance at least sometimes, you will make your life easier.

You must do your best to rein in any inclination to dominate other people's lives and to direct them; and to fight off the usually unnecessary feelings of jealousy you experience from intense relationships of love, and in friendships. Your emotions, once engaged, can run deep. You love companionship, and party wildly when you're in the mood, but some people still perceive you as emotionally cool. This means you sometimes spend too much time on your own. You must work to communicate your real needs to friends and lovers, for they can't be expected to read your often deep and complex personality. You know you like to come first with everyone – but there is always room for others in the landscape too. If you can listen to advice, without always feeling it's a sign of weakness to do so, you can later reject any ideas which don't fit in with your vision: it is illuminating to listen others, even when you don't always agree.

As you have a logical mind you should be able to separate your emotions from your intellect and make objective decisions. You are practical and powerful, idealistic and imaginative. This gives you a huge range of career options, which we'll look at in more detail later, but the following ideas are most strongly suited to your individual birthday on the 1st.

You have a gift for dynamic and inspirational teaching of any kind, and you also love acting – enjoying the independence and originality of individual roles, as well as savouring the moment alone in the spotlight. You have a talent for any work connected with inventing, and – perhaps not unrelated – for designing. This includes fashion, architecture, design technology and computer programming, although some of these would work best if they were supported by the number **4** anywhere else in your numbers – such as a predominance of the letters D and M in your name. The letters F, O and X (relating to the number **6**) in your name, in conjunction with your particular birthday, would bolster your natural facility with fashion or other creative arts.

But, whatever else, you definitely need to work independently and be left to your own devices without interruption, so that you are allowed to follow your own train of thought and imagination to its conclusion. You have a huge capacity for focus to get things going, and are an entrepreneur of sorts, quite prepared to live in very basic conditions while you're in start-up mode.

Born on the 10th?

Your birthday shares many similarities to the 1st because it contains just the pure digit '1' – although in this instance the zero increases some tendencies tenfold. You are equally independent and self-reliant as someone born on the 1st, sometimes bossy (admit it!), and you naturally assume the lead even in adverse circumstances. Your energies are aggressive in a *positive* way; yours is a voice to be heard, and you're a force to be reckoned with. You will never allow yourself to be treated like a doormat.

It is likely that you work alone, or in your own business – and probably not in a nine-to-five routine. You will go out of your way to create variety or build in room for the unexpected. You have such adrenaline rushes of energy that you are more than able to work an outrageously extended day – as long as you are absorbed in what is going on. You are idealistic, full of clever ideas about how to improve the world around you, and you initiate changes at work and in your home. You love to find fresh approaches to stale situations, and you push everyone to their maximum potential, until they have exerted themselves to the full. You may even be able to manage more than one business at a time, or follow various strands of endeavour simultaneously. This helps you to bring at least one project close to your heart to fruition, even if some others go nowhere.

In your case it is a strength that you are both able and willing to stand on your own, for throughout your life people will have leaned on you heavily, and come looking for your brand of courage and boldness. Others instinctively seek your advice, but are less sure how to help you if you need it. They perceive you as entirely self-sufficient – not always accurately – and admire your strength of character.

You have original ideas and perhaps even unusual

morals in regard to life and the way to do business. You take cues from no one, finding out your mistakes through hard-earned knocks, but you wear your scars with some pride. You may prefer to go it alone most of the time, and you are surprisingly shy of asking for what you want from anyone else – even from your partner. Ergo, you do the job all yourself.

You are not always sensible about how hard you push yourself, nor are you good at taking orders from others. Though you and the '28's are the most gentle of the **1**s, you are nevertheless more stubborn than anyone about the way to try something, and you like to follow your own advice. We will be looking in detail at your career potential later, but as an overview specific to your birthday, some paths especially shine out for you. Business is in itself a possible career choice – perhaps running a personnel company, or managing a corporation. If you have a lot of 'D's or 'M's in your name, or your **LIFE** number is **4** (which we will see later), property development and management would suit you.

You are certainly gifted in many directions, though may have begun to pursue several talents and then lost the urge to complete or polish any of them. Music, painting and architecture are fields in which you could shine, but you crave variety, so may not settle at any one of these (although the absence of regular work hours they often entail would be bliss for you). You naturally re-invent everyday items to make them more exciting. You are sharp-minded but not always tolerant of others, and intellectually original and attracted to new ideas. Very strong-minded, you are remarkably jealous of your possessions and friends. Many women born on this birth date are not only fiercely independent and strong, but also lack any inclination to act out the 'traditional' role of female domesticity. This means you will find interesting ways of making love partnerships work for you.

Born on the 19th?

You are an old soul. **1** people are often thought of as fresh and young on the karmic ladder, but if you believe in such things, *your* number is uniquely one that suggests that many lifetimes of learning and growth have come before this one.

This birthday carries wonderful artistic talents and creative urges, a very original sense of humour, and an ability to weave these two aspects of your character together to create new trends wherever you go. But the previous lifetimes may also include lessons you are still discharging, from mistakes you have made: you perhaps have some things to learn harking back to another life, and may be asked to stand alone much more than you wish – again and again – from your childhood until your oldest age. Fortunately, you really do have the strength to cope with this, but it will sometimes seem a lot to ask, and you will never feel you have a free ride.

Your number is associated with emotional extremes, partly because of the very *feeling* quality of the number **9**, which is in your date, and you may find yourself vacillating between an exuberant optimism and a moody pessimism on different days. You will have to be determined not to indulge in wallowing in the depths of despair for too long whenever there is an inevitable test or setback. Remember: you have immense intelligence and great charm when you want to draw on it, which can always help you through tight corners. And, in fact, you love challenges, and like to keep on your toes.

You cherish private time, and resent too much intrusion from company, but when you are in the mood for entertaining friends no one is a better or funnier host. You will push hard to improve many of the conditions of your existence, and you have excellent and unique ideas to offer. People may think you mad sometimes, but – usually – you have the last laugh.

Like all the different **1**s, you can be nervous and irritable or quick to anger, but you are just as quick to recover your temper, and perhaps the most forgiving of the **1**s when others raise your ire. You set yourself very high standards to live by, and often have rather traditional moral views – considering the originality of other aspects of your personality. And you usually expect those closest to you to follow suit. Thus you are sometimes in danger of missing out on complete happiness in relationships, partly because of a reflex instinct to withdraw into your own little world, and appear thoroughly self-sufficient. Do some people read this as self-centred instead? You can be misunderstood because of this trait, and you will need to find a way of articulating what it is that you need or desire.

A full career section follows shortly, but your precise birthday has some special versatilities. You could succeed in different fields over the course of your life, or at least try your hand at more than one profession. The '9' in your number means that part of you wants to be in the lime-light, but another part wants to work privately, unwatched, within your own areas of interest. In both cases, though, you will be happiest working for yourself, or, if you are part of a large company, you will need the freedom to arrive at – and act on – your own decisions. You should be left to your own devices as far as circumstances can allow. You won't let your team down, and laziness is not one of your failings.

Your particular career choices include politics and law, sometimes medicine, and physically demanding jobs like dance, sport (all those hours of training alone suit you), all types of design, and teaching at a high level. You love to work strange hours, and you need new challenges from time to time.

Born on the 28th?

With the marriage of the numbers **2** and **8** to make your version of **1**, you are perhaps more able to read and intuit others' needs than any other **1** birthday. This date makes you a true individual, and symbolizes very high ideals and perfection of standards.

Though you do have a huge self-will and independent nature, you also have a capacity for really deep affection once it has been bestowed on someone. This sets you apart from other **1**s, and the '2' makes you considerate of your partner's needs. You are still quite private and dominant, and you need no one to sanction your actions and beliefs, but for a **1** you are uniquely able to sacrifice some of your drive to self-sufficiency for the sake of emotional contentment, and you are able to fit ambition and relationship together more successfully than many **1**s.

As '2' is feminine and '8' sees two sides to everything, your relationships and friendships are sometimes quite unconventional. You certainly love very sincerely, but you will love whomever you will, with or without family approval! You are a 'chancer', a maker and taker of opportunities, and as such an especially charismatic partner. You start lots of projects, and know when to delegate so that other more suitable people may finish them. This offsets the chance that you will lose interest anyway, once things are up and running.

Big expansive '8' ambitions yoked to your '1' drive mean that you must have freedom and that you rail at limitations – particularly if they are put in place by inferior or more cautious intellects. You are single-minded, and can wait quite patiently until the time is ripe to propel yourself into action, which certainly isn't the case for those with other '1' birthdays. You sometimes magnify your problems beyond the reality of their impact, so you should guard against this kind of exaggeration and not let it lead to insecurity or self-delusion. It is also possible that you can, at times, lapse into laziness or too much arrogance and conceit. Don't waste too much time on the dreaming-up phase of your plans, for your destiny is to achieve results that other **1**s lack the drive to accomplish.

As a prequel to the career section which follows this, your birthday sets you up perfectly for success as a leader, an executive, the affable and enthusiastic spokesperson asked to spearhead new projects. Your '1' makes you fully prepared to stand alone if need be, and ready to assert your rights as well as those of others, but your '2' and '8' together additionally help you to understand others' reservations, and you seem to work hard to resolve their difficulties. This makes you the *capo di capi*: among a group of independent thinkers, you will be the leader.

You teach people under you well, and you may choose this as a career, but you will expect both dedication and excellence from your students. You may also be drawn to law, or some kind of self-employment. Any vocation which demands physical energy will work for you. Fascinatingly, the 28th has been the birthday of many kings.

1 AT WORK

So, what kind of employee does your number make you? We've already seen that your birthday suggests you are much more comfortable working for yourself than for someone else, but when you're in a group, how do you fit in? If you're the boss, are you a good one? Which fields are likely to be the best for your talents? And which the worst? And what about the male/female divide? Is a 1 female boss more desirable than a 1 male colleague?

Here, we get to grips with your career potential, your needs and 'must-have's for job satisfaction, and your loves and loathes work-wise, hopefully highlighting some areas where there is room for you to adjust your manner around others, to help you achieve what it is you're aiming for.

In the marketplace

Your number, as we have said, is the 'I am' of numerology, rather like the first Fire sign of the zodiac, Aries. This means that, whether as corporation owner or floor-worker on the way up, you are aware always of the *self* at the centre of the world around you, with a heightened sense of your own desires and a driving feeling of what you must do for your own self-preservation.

This may not sound entirely flattering, but it is also not altogether a bad thing, either. In the Darwinian world of struggle, **1**s are the survivors – although in a society which recognizes the desirability of achieving a harmonious community, you should never let your instinct for promoting the self devolve into unalloyed selfishness.

WHERE YOU LEAD

Career-wise, then, the best word through which to understand your **1** id is 'leadership'. Regardless of the field of expression you choose to work in, or the vocation life seems to thrust at you, your character will announce its fitness for leading where others must follow. Even if you work among equals in a low-profile atmosphere, when there is a crisis or pressured situation that demands a swift response, you will come naturally to the fore and calm those around you who are flailing. Oddly enough, **1** people frequently go into meltdown when the milk spills from the refrigerator or the telephone lines go down, but are cool as cucumbers in a serious crisis, which is why others always look to you as a beacon to follow in a storm.

In any work you do, your independent initiative and instinct for what may work will see you reach high levels of success – which is why **1**s never stay below management level for long. Equally, the ability to take charge of all jobs and the need to be in the driving seat is what forces so many **1**s into their own business – or, at least, into a partnership that gives them free rein in their sector.

WHERE DOES YOUR LIGHT REALLY SHINE?

Here are some of the qualities that **1**s bring to any job:

- Keen perception and good concentration mean you are always likely to get ahead, but you're especially likely to establish a successful business of your own if you desire it. Other talented people will join you where you lead.
- You have executive ability, which means you can overcome any obstacle that threatens to derail a project or venture. Your courage and originality help you solve difficulties others can't negotiate.
- You like to have the finer things in life, which drives you to select – as far as possible – a high-paying career that will guarantee you appropriate rewards for your effort. You are not averse to a system of bonuses paid for extra

achievement, as this suits the way you work.

- The policy you live by – of never allowing life to become dull – pushes you to excel at what you do, and makes you naturally attracted to interesting work that has a varied menu from day to day. The minute a job becomes routine, you will leave it!
- You don't take orders easily from others – not even from those you respect.

All of these make you a person with unlimited skills and options. Where certain numbers have just one or two really clear lines of endeavour in which they will fly high, you can make a success of almost any course of work that allows you the kind of scope outlined above.

In any vocational path which demands that you develop new contacts, clients or projects, you are in your element. Careers that work well with this kind of talent include ...

Design: fashion/interior/graphic You have the nerve to take chances and break from the rules, and you see what the market will want ahead of its time. You also know how to recruit a team of people to make up for any of your own shortfalls in actual artistic ability or ability to calculate costs. Bold colours are attractive to you, so you will experiment with them rather than continue beating a familiar path.

Property management and development Real estate interests you, and you love the freedom of ranging from place to place as part of your work day. You see what can be done with a site or in a location – and frequently design its finished look as well. Female **1**s especially will prosper in this field.

Publishing Originating something is the challenge you jump to, and in this field you also enjoy contributing as an illustrator, writer or promoter of new titles and types of work. Whatever you are drawn to in publishing, you are sure to find new ways of doing things, and be known as an innovator within your spectrum.

Government No, not a civil servant, but the front-runner! You love to wrangle with authority for the sake of making change and forcing progress in this world, and you also love the spotlight. Many leading politicians, past and present, have a number **1** birthday.

Teaching and public speaking These are both careers which demand natural leaders. Your good brain and memory help you execute the demands of these jobs adroitly.

Inventors Yes, it's obvious after all that you've read about yourself so far, but the DAY number **1** is ideally suited to a life of inventing – even if that means working within a larger company and finding ways to re-invent things to make them better.

Health industry – especially medicine or surgery The long hours are a killer for mere mortals, but a **1** will easily cope with this demand. The variety of work is a bonus, and the sense of being in control and of being 'on your own in a crunch' is perfect for you. Again, the excellent memory and get-ahead, competitive mentality ensures success if this is your chosen field.

If your companion (LIFE) number is **7**, you will be likely to specialize or do research; whereas if it's **6**, or if you have the letters F, O or X dominant in your name, you will be extremely good with patients and counselling the sick (*see* LIFE-*number section, page 214*).

Art Whether fine art or antiques, art often entices the interests of a **1** – partly because it allows you solitude to work creating art or rescuing antiques, but also because you are drawn to the beauty or uniqueness of a piece.

IT The computer world isn't boring for you, as you create new uses and applications for the technology. You may be skilled at writing new programmes, or just running a business from your computer – the flexible hours being right up your street.

Drama, cinema, TV You are at home in media-related jobs because of their tremendous potential for trying new things and reaching large numbers of people. Where many are drawn to the buzz of this industry but worried by the lack of security or fear of going freelance, this registers as a 'plus' in the column of challenges for a **1**. Directors, writers and actors all find safe haven in this area, and enjoy the unusual pattern of work hours it entails.

This list isn't exhaustive – a **1** can thrive in so many different career paths, as long as they offer freedom and the chance to work independently – but it does offer a taste of what kind of field suits your number.

And for luck?

Whatever your work, you will achieve your maximum potential if you use a name to work with that includes the letter A, J or S. Remember this when you are choosing a company name, if you go into business for yourself. It will help, too, for you to optimize your energy and positive attitude, if you decorate your work environment in the coppery colours of sunrise: flame, scarlet and apricot yellow-reds. If you are going for an important interview, these colours would make a positive choice in your outfit, as they help you to project yourself in your strongest light.

WORK PROFILE

The 1 female boss

Distinctively dressed, usually **physically fit**, and often all leggy and fabulous, the **1** female in charge of her business brood is a fierce **mother tigress**. She exudes quiet, **authoritative** energy across the office floor, and her highly individual scent lingers in both the ladies room and at the conference table. Even the men she works with as equals give her **respect**, and may even secretly be slightly afraid of her.

Her desk may not be luxurious, for she is unwilling to waste time on anything deemed unnecessary, but she has **signature touches** that announce to visitors that they are in her domain. Her sunrise colours – of reds and fiery golds – are in evidence around her. Her conversations with clients and international peers are **brief** but not rude, and she is always hurrying to another appointment or running out of town. If she is late for a meeting she will **waltz** into the boardroom, floating fabric – perhaps a scarf – trailing behind her, and never offer an apology. Miraculously, no one seems to mind, for she **sets the scene** in her own unique way and gives one hundred and fifty per cent of herself at the gathering. Tell her something once and she'll never forget it, and trust her to be **on her game** and have every fact at her fingertips when she has to impress.

The **1** female boss is a **hard act to follow**, and will always get a brilliant performance from her co-workers. As long as they follow her lead!

WORK PROFILE

The 1 male boss

Sometimes less of a peacock than his female counterpart, the **1** male running his establishment is nevertheless clearly **at the helm**. Touches of his personality, once you know it, are evident from the front door right through to the top of the building. He likes to have original people around him, and he controls them with **surprising largesse**, for he knows he will get the best performance from his team if they are allowed to develop things quietly. He would expect this courtesy himself.

When you meet him he is **attentive** to all you say – almost; but his mind is managing the clever feat of **skipping ahead** to the next thing he wants to introduce, or working out where this all could lead to six months from now. His dress style is distinctive and not always à la mode, but **distinguishing marks** of his eccentricity are probably for a trained eye or those who know him very well. The red socks will be there, or the red tie, but not at the expense of a well-cut suit or an expensive shirt. Throw every new idea you can at him and he will give you **audience**: moreover, he will **reward** your initiative, for he was like you once, and he hasn't forgotten.

Of course, ultimately there is only one way to do things, and that's **his way**. But others who watch will learn a great deal from a **1** man in charge; his dictionary doesn't include the word 'impossible', so life working with this man will be **exciting**, daring and **fascinating** – even if those around him have to learn to be a little circumspect at times. **Bossy**? Yes, he is – but that's partly his job!

WORK PROFILE

The 1 female employee

You noticed her the first day she arrived, with her pot plant and her own distinctive coffee cup and her very daring wallpaper on her PC. But if you think she's in her own world, think again. She has an ear on everything happening around the workplace, and she will soon know everyone's secrets and anxieties. Not that she will break a confidence – she has a **strong sense of ethics** about this. Just expect a **1** employee, however, to **know exactly what's going on** around her, and to bide her time until such knowledge is a help to her in influencing her actions.

She is **loyal** but she is **competitive**, and she is not going to be working for someone else for too long. This is a girl **on the way up**, and she knows how to use her considerable assets to get there. She doesn't have to be asked to do anything twice, and she will volunteer to do the messiest jobs to further a cause and, incidentally, to **get noticed**. She learns quickly, and soon evolves her own style. She has good ideas and brings a **freshness** to her working space, like opening a window. **Self-reliant**, she shows initiative whenever she can, and will soon be putting more senior members of the team to shame, and making it clear that she is **prepared to learn anything** new to grow in the job. It's pointless telling her how to do things: she will **find her own way**, whatever you suggest.

She's likely to be very feminine, but with a very masculine outlook – blurring the boundaries of what's supposed to be what in the business. But watch her ... because she is definitely going to **succeed**.

WORK PROFILE

The 1 male employee

Not one to get left behind by the female **1** in the other corner, this is someone with **charm** and **wit**, and what he lacks in sophistication he makes up in energy and **ambition**. The **1** male in a subordinate job is **biding time** until his world opens into new vistas, but until then you have someone who has his eyes and ears open and his memory-bank **alert**.

His dress lacks refinement possibly, but he is distinctive and generates a **sex appeal** all his own. If his ideas are not heeded by his superiors he will become **grumpy** and frustrated, for he is an ideas man, but he is happy enough being a team player for a while, as long as he feels appreciated for his spark and **originality**. His desk is sometimes (not always) a mess because he is dwelling in the world of ideas, **thinking ahead** to the future. He is funny and **good company**, but relationships don't always run smoothly for him as he likes his time to himself at weekends. Commitment-phobic? Up to a point, but he wants to get his career on track first, anyhow.

Ask him to do menial tasks at your peril, because this is not the best he has to offer, and you will blunt his **willingness**. He is a **natural leader** when delegation has to take place, so throw your worst at him and be amazed at the way he handles tough assignments. He can stay up late or work into the night, and he is ready to travel to sub-zero temperatures at an hour's notice if it means he will get further up the ladder himself. Challenge him, trust his **diligence**, but don't ignore him or get in his way. He has **places to go**, and he's in a hurry.

Ideal world or cruel world?

Best and worst jobs ...

IN AN IDEAL WORLD

Best job for a 1 female: Head of arts programming for a TV station (responsibility, variety, creativity, recognition for achievement)

Best job for a 1 male: Transport co-ordinator for a space mission (varied, crazy hours, dangerous at times, envied by others)

IN A CRUEL WORLD

Worst job for a 1 female: Manager of a garbage recycling plant (responsibility, repetitiveness, no creativity, low sense of personal status)

Worst job for a 1 male: Personal assistant to an actor or famous author (always answerable to someone else and never being the star!)

1'S CHILDHOOD

Seeing the way a number expresses itself in someone very young is fascinating, for the tendencies and responses are all in their infancy – and yet plain to see. Some facets of a number's power need to be grown into, and take time to reveal how they will be dealt with by the developing character. Sometimes the strength of a number can be a frustration when we're young.

If looking back on your own childhood through the lens of your number, you should discover – with considerable humour and irony – a renewed understanding of some of the difficulties or excitements you experienced. Or, if you have a child who is also a **1**, you may learn something more useful; it is an advantage to understand the qualities a number exudes over an awakening personality, especially in relation to talents and career strengths, as it might save a lot of frustrations. You'll be able to appreciate the positive traits, and handle negative ones more sympathetically.

Here, we take a detailed look at what it's like to be a child bearing your number. But what about the other numbers? Perhaps you have a child who is a **6**, and you'd like to know what that means? Or maybe you'd like to gain insight into friends' and siblings' childhoods, to see if it sheds any light on the people they have become today? A short profile is given for each number, along with advice for a **1** parent on dealing with other-number offspring.

Just as your own parents would have discovered when you yourself were a child, the hardest thing with a **1** child is getting them to obediently follow anything you dictate! **1**s, as you know, like to assert their independence and learn everything for themselves, and are not always happy to take direction ...

The young 1

A child born on the 1st, 10th, 19th or 28th is very resourceful when it comes to their belief system, right from the earliest age. Read something from a children's book, or repeat Grandma's sound advice on any subject to a **1** under the age of six, and they'll simply ask, 'Why?' This child has a different way of thinking and is perfectly ready to stand to one side and evaluate things without pressure. The social expectation to conform is less of a problem for someone with this number, even when they are very young. A **1** child creates their own vocabulary, their own moral convictions, their own look, their own highly unusual role models and viewpoints. **1** children often make us laugh with surprise.

A **1** child – at least until puberty – is tough and physically active, often sporty, energetic, quick to comprehend, and an inquisitive soul who wants to get on with things and not be held in check by others, however wise the parental eye might be. Does this mean stubborn and impatient? Definitely – and a **1** child frequently suffers by questioning the authority of a parent or teacher, rather than meekly toeing the line. This, though, is not done out of rudeness, but as a matter of breaking down tradition and finding new ideas and reasons, to form a fresh understanding of the world we're in. Many adults find themselves put on the spot by intelligent questions fired from enthusiastic young **1**s – and it's a personality trait that will grow stronger over time!

It could be a lonely road, but a **1** child is always aware of their inner strength and 'apart-ness', and relishes the fact that they stand out from the crowd. It's how they like things to be. When a **1** is dressed in a style similar to their siblings, they will find a way to alter the length of their coat or hitch their dress up higher with a belt; they will wear anything with individuality.

1's toys

Telescope • Chess board • Artist's brushes and paints • Kite • Tent and sleeping bag • Racing cars (for 1 boys *and* girls!) • Solo musical instrument

In childhood, **1**s need careful handling. A bright mind bursting with interest – with a disinclination towards authority – needs subtle direction. The task is to help them discover their enviable self-worth and encourage that ground-breaking unconventional view of life while persuading them away from outright selfishness or arrogance. If the tendency to dominate their friends and talk over their family is not chided at times, it can cause **1**s to be altogether bombastic socially, and unable to co-operate in love relationships later in life, and this will lead to loneliness rather than just self-reliance. A **1** child's willpower is a plus-point, but their boredom threshold will be an issue. They need to be set fresh challenges by adults and teachers, and allowed scope for exploration to channel their enthusiasm.

A **1**'s greatest challenge through life – and it's a journey which begins at the cradle – is to learn to live in a social world and to understand that they are not inevitably right on all scores. To help them build a unique personality and avoid insensitivity to others it is therefore best to allow them, as far as possible, to behave like an adult. This is a confidence a **1** child will ably repay. They need time to be heard, space for their ideas to be tested, and an audience to consider their unexpected observations.

Just as **1**s suffer in adulthood from being misunderstood, a **1** child often seems so happy in their private hours and so demanding of having their own time that they may not learn to express their need for others. It is often a danger that **1**s – from toddler to teen – project their self-confidence so strongly that their need for a hug or for support is overlooked. The seeds are sown early as to how to approach another person for signs of affection, so a canny parent might simply wade in across the private moat and cover their **1** child with kisses when the time seems to demand it. **1**s need just such an intuitive parent or partner to do this, but if they have a mum or dad who has a strong personality, chances are they will respect this show of equal power and come out of their prickly private zone.

A **1** child has, perhaps, almost too much to give, but it doesn't always seem that way. The lesson for a **1** child (even in adulthood) is to be patient with their parents, who are sometimes slower on the uptake; and the lesson for a parent of a **1** child is to not be afraid of offering their explorer-child some parameters. Everyone will be happier for it.

The 2 child

All children born on the 2nd or 20th need affection and a peaceful environment to grow up in. Those born on the 11th or 29th are a little different, being master number **11**s with **2** as the denominator, and they have an old head on young shoulders from the beginning of their lives. But even they – for all their drive toward excitement and adventure – will be happiest if their home life is mostly secure and tranquil.

These highly sensitive and intuitive children know what you will say before you say it. They are also dreamy and process ideas in their sleep, waking to instinctive and wise solutions to their problems. But they are vulnerable, and need reassuring more than most numbers. They are acutely sensitive to criticism, feeling that all comments are proof that they're not quite good enough, so you need to deliver your words with tact and an awareness of their needs.

2 children are talented artists, actors, dancers and/or musicians: they know how others *feel*. A **2** child prefers to support friends and family as often as possible, and this can make them a doormat ready to be walked on unless those they live with are alert to their inclinations. If the **2** is an **11**, the wish to help out will be very strong indeed, but these children also have a finely tuned moral sense and will be offended by injustice – especially against them! Don't dish out judgement until you have all the facts.

All **2**s are good healers and can make others feel better – even from their earliest years. Knowing when to cuddle or touch and when to be quiet, they often have a stillness which works miracles around the sick, the sad and the elderly. A **1** parent with a **2** child must be careful not to ignore their input or talk across them, nor be impatient with them – and must also not forget how much joy and support they receive from their gentle, intelligent **2** child.

The 3 child

From the cradle, **3**s hold parties and like to mix with other children. They have a capacity to laugh and precipitate laughter, even when things go a little wrong. **3** children are like the reappearing sun after rain, and their energies can be restorative for everyone. Creative and playful, nothing keeps them low for long.

Like a juggler keeping plates and balls in the air, **3**s have several activities and talents on the go from the start. This can be a problem, however: making decisions is hard for them, and they need a wise older counsellor who can talk out the options and give them room to think. Even then, a decision once reached can always be changed – and a **3** child will find a way to run in several directions at one time.

Keep your **3** busy with lots of artistic activities, using colours and textures – right from babyhood – to open their eyes to what they can do. Even before the age of ten a strong personal taste will begin to develop – and it may not be the same as their parents'. Using up their flow of energy on a multitude of tasks will be demanding on both parents, but the **3** child does give a great deal back in return.

3s are talkers and have a witty repartee, even when tiny: you'll be surprised at what you hear from them sometimes, and will wonder where it came from. Naturally gifted at PR, they will talk you around when you are set against one of their wishes, but you will need to direct them now and again or nothing will ever be finished! A **1** parent with a **3** child must allow them scope to try things differently, and not be upset if they are sometimes messy or chatter too much. Draw clear lines for them to follow, and they will always come up smiling.

The 4 child

Surprisingly insecure and in need of praise, these children are reliable and hard-working and want to do well. They are their own worst critics at times, second only to number **7** children, and they glow when appreciated. They are happiest with family around them – even extended members – and often prefer holidays in familiar places. That said, they can be very quiet and self-sufficient when required, for they concentrate well.

These are organized children who won't cope well if their parents aren't as organized as they are! Never lose a school form or an item from their games kit on a crucial day, as this will cause them serious panic. They like to have material possessions around them because this bolsters their feeling of security, and will manage their pocket money well, content to do odd jobs and chores to gain this reward.

4s love the earth and buildings. They will treasure a patch of garden given them to tend, or a garden house they can extend or build outright. If they are born on the 22nd, rather than the 4th, 13th or 31st, they will truly have architectural talents, and may follow design as a career later. All **4** children, though, are handy at craft work and excellent at projects which require intelligence combined with method to get something done. They hate being late and don't admire tardiness in others, either.

As children, **4**s are loyal and dependable to family and friends, and are more patient than many numbers. They will make light of complex tasks, but they need to be allowed to do things in their own way. A **1** parent may consider their **4** child unimaginative or, occasionally, plodding; but they simply have a different approach to the duties of life. **4**s feel more responsible towards others, where **1**s are brave and, at times, foolhardy. This leads to stubborn clashes, but **4**s soon learn to stand fast through **1**'s storm-bursts.

The 5 child

Unable to be confined or to sit still, a **5** child is bursting with curiosity about life and people. Very sociable and happy to be on the move, these adventurous youngsters have much in common with **1**s, but are more willing to work in a team, and good at picking up on other people's ideas, only to improve them.

From their first few words, **5** children have good memories and a facility for speech – they speak and learn quickly, and can pick up more than one language. Even more physical than **1**s (although the two numbers are alike in this), they are excellent at sport or physical co-ordination. They chatter, are full of energy, and like to play to an audience. But most importantly, **5** children love to be free – to explore, laze, hunt, create, discover and travel. Take your **5** child away on holiday and they quickly make friends with others, and acquire a taste for foreign places. They will even experiment with different food, if you're lucky.

5s find a reason to slip away if they're bored with adult company – so don't be offended. Their minds can pursue several streams of active interest, so they need a great deal of amusement to stretch them. This adventurous spirit can be a worry to their family sometimes and, indeed, **5**s need to understand house rules about asking first, or telling someone where they're off to. The difficulty is that **5** children usually don't want to explain themselves to anyone.

The test for a **5**'s parent is to set their child constructive challenges that will vent their curiosity in good ways. **5**s will pick up technology and music (other forms of language, in a sense) quickly, but they don't like dull routine work – which will irritate a **4** sibling if they have one. A **1** parent of a **5** child should be proud of their offspring, as they show initiative and are quick on the uptake. But, arguments about freedom to roam will be a problem.

The 6 child

Here's a young soul in need of a peaceful haven, just like a **2**, but a **6** will literally feel ill if there is dissension around them. Always wanting to beautify their surroundings and make pretty presents for Mum, these talented, sensitive children have many gifts for creative expression. They will also nurse the sick cat or anyone who needs gentle kindness, but are not always robust themselves, and should be sheltered from bad weather or aggressive viruses.

As children, **6**'s musical talents should emerge – and they often have beautiful speaking or singing voices. They are also the peacemakers of the family – natural creators of balance and harmony. Give them a free hand with their bedroom and their flower garden, and be ready to learn from them. Both boys and girls usually make good cooks when they are older, too, so time spent in the kitchen won't be wasted. Birthday presents that foster their good eye – a camera or set of art tools – will usually fit them well.

Despite being sensitive to others and quite intuitive, **6** as a child is a little shy and needs drawing out – especially if there has been much change in their young life, because **6** children need stability and like to remain a tiny bit traditional. They become very attached to their home. But if their family life is unconventional they will ultimately adjust, because they offer their family a lot of love, and like to be shown love in return. Even the boys have a feminine side which in no way calls their gender into question.

Good at school and almost as well-organized as **4**s, this is a number which needs time to grow into itself: **6**s really are enormously talented. A **1** parent must be gentle with a **6**, who is not as confident as the leading number. But when a **1** needs a friend to listen, support, encourage, back them up, they will often find unsuspected reservoirs of strength in this interesting child.

The 7 child

Even in primary school this is a child with a focused mind and a strongly developed critical sense. A **7** child is perceptive and, sometimes, disarmingly quiet. They will often prefer adult company, as their peers will probably seem too young and underdeveloped to them. Wise and difficult to know well, these are children with a serious cast to their intelligent minds.

The fact that a **7** child can sit quietly and contemplate things deeply should not imply that they are introverted: quite the opposite. A **7** will grow into a very good host as long as the company appeals, and they have a lovely sense of humour, apparent from their earliest years – even if it does sometimes find expression at others' expense. They will rarely be rude, but certainly have a good understanding of all that has been said – and what has not been.

Listen to their impressions of the people they deal with!

All **7**s as children have an inward reluctance to accept other people's ideas automatically – rather like **1**s – but there is a special propensity to independence in a child born on the 16th. This is the number of someone who finds it difficult asking for what they want – someone who often feels as though they haven't been consulted as to their own wishes. And all **7**s certainly have definite ideas about what to believe.

7 children should be told the truth on virtually all matters; they will know if they are being deceived, and will respect being treated as an adult in any case. A **1** parent will understand this, as they feel similarly about fostering early strengths. **1** and **7** are closely related to one another, and both like privacy and personal space. A parent and child with these numbers should grow close and become a good team.

The 8 child

Here we have a young executive in the making. Even when they are still at school these children have a canny nose for what will make good business – and yet they are generous, hard-working and prepared to learn everything it will take to succeed in this life. Children born on the 8th, 17th and 26th like to have charge of their own finances, and to be given scope to do 'grown-up' activities – organizing their own parties and making arrangements for outings with their friends.

These children have strength and energy, but mentally are reflective and wise, too. They always see both sides to an argument – so parents who ask them to choose sides, beware! An **8** makes good judgements, and even before the age of ten they have a sense of what is fair and what is morally right.

As this number rules the octave, many **8** children are extremely musical and have a wonderful sense of rhythm. This last even assures they can be good at sport, as it takes innate timing to perfect many physical skills. **8**s also like philosophical ideas and relish being given 'big concepts' to chew over, especially concerning politics or religious ideas. **8**s are proud, and like to research things carefully – so as long as they are not bored, you will find an **8** child with their head in a book or on the internet, or watching programmes that educate and broaden their vistas.

Try to understand that an **8** is always striving for balance, and this will help you to be pragmatic if they are sometimes pulling in the opposite direction from you. **8**s are loyal to those they love, but a delicate sensibility makes them also look at the other side of a story, or fight for an underdog. But as a **1** parent you understand the urge to go it alone when necessary, and – mostly – you will respect the qualities and mind of your **8** child.

The 9 child

Here is a person born for the theatre, or to travel the world and befriend everyone. **9**s have an expansive view of things, and don't like to be restricted. With a good head for both science and the arts, there are many career directions a **9** may take, so parents will have their work cut out trying to help them choose. However, because the number **9** is like a mirror, with every number added to it reducing again to that same number (for example: 5+9 = 14, and 1+4 = 5), **9** children are able to take on the feelings of just about anyone, which is why they are so artistic and good at drama and writing.

From their first years in school it will be clear a **9** child has a wonderful dry sense of humour and a taste for the unusual. **9** children are not often prejudiced and seem to be easy-going – though they are sensitive to the atmosphere around them, picking up vibes like a sponge. If you speak to them harshly, they will take it seriously and are protective of others who seem to be hurt in this way too.

9s have a delicate relationship with their parents, but particularly with the father figure. A **9** girl will want to idolize her dad, and will feel desperately disappointed if circumstances are against this, while a **9** boy may wish to emulate his father – and yet they often grow up without enough input from this important person, who is busy or away. A **9** child must be wise ahead of their time, and so this lesson is thrown at them in one guise or another.

A **1** parent of a **9** child must be circumspect. The **1** has such raw energy and drive that the child often finds it offensive and unrefined. **9** would rather contemplate and consider what is to be done, and this basic personality difference must be worked through. Together, however, they can start and finish almost anything, so a partnership is much the best option.

1 AT PLAY

We have discovered how your number expresses itself through your character in relation to your family and your general personality, what instinctive reactions go with your number in everyday situations, and how it might shape your career path and colour your childhood. But every day our DAY number also influences the way we respond to the social world around us. So, what can it say about our leisure hours? Is yours a number that even allows itself to relax? (Well, you probably already have some answers to this one!) What can your number reveal about the way you like to spend your time, or how you achieve pleasure outside of duty?

Over the next few pages we take a look at what makes you tick, as a **1**, when you are unwinding – and how **1**s prefer to fill their time, if given a choice. Let's see whether you're typical in this respect ... And who knows – if you haven't already tried all the activities and pastimes mentioned, maybe you'll get a few ideas about what to put on your list for next time!

The 1 woman at play

As you well know, yours is a number that is not naturally at ease when expected to conform to domestic gender roles, or if you are ever forced to be housebound; and you know very well that you can be competitive, enjoy sports and like the thrill of winning. It follows, then, that these qualities have a part to play when it comes to how you spend your private time.

You are not always romantic in the conventional sense (and we will say much more about this when we come to the section on love), but you have a willingness to be swept off your feet by anyone – even friends – when it comes to doing any activity impromptu. Five minutes' notice to pack is fine – or, more likely, you will be the one making that phonecall to arrange such a last-minute outing when a friend or lover is in need. *You* are the one to break the pattern of previous behaviour, start a new trend or mine a new vein of riches; and so it is in your own time.

You will relish the chance to get off the main tourist path when you're on holiday, or to go to a tiny place in the mountains where no tourist guide has been. You love colourful places and people, and you are physically hardy enough, in general, to take yourself on an adventure. You will find life dull if you are asked to 'chill out' in a spa for days on end, but you'll set off on a path no matter where it might take you or what you may meet along it. And when you head for a walk in the country, you take the lead – and your companions will have to stretch to keep up with you.

A beach holiday can have its appeal, provided it offers a chance for you to think quietly without a friend muttering at you. Huge horizons open up your creative thoughts, so staring at the skyline can be a prop for your imagination. If a friend recommends a venue, you are more likely to find somewhere they've never been: a **1** woman repeats other people's behaviour rarely, instead finding new places of interest. An action holiday suits you well, usually, and many **1**s set off in striking ski-wear or on deep-sea diving expeditions, to combine their physical courage and energy with a chance to think in a fathomless place.

You can enjoy doing things to your home – but not in the sense of keeping house! **1** women spending a week's holiday at home are likely to completely change their environment, becoming bored if there is no movement in their life. Inspiration comes from all sorts of places, and, as long as it is different and original, you are happy. If your attention moves to the garden, you are likely to be the designer of the space and leave the elbow work to hired professionals. This is not because you are afraid of the hard work – far from it – but the challenge is in envisioning, not completing, the project. You will have moved on to the bedroom or the bathroom by the time the work is done.

If it's not something you do for a living, then designing or painting is often a hobby for the **1** woman. Or you like to visit galleries and see the latest movies – anything that is up to the minute. It is not unusual for you to take a course in a free week or over a long weekend, just to keep your clever mind keened. You can relax, but relaxation for you is more often the release of adrenaline than the sitting and contemplating of the world indefinitely.

The 1 man at play

You are even more competitive than a **1** woman (if this is possible!), and you love to spend your days off honing your skills. Speed is one of your best friends, and a **1** man is the smiling recipient of a gift experience spent at a car racing track or canoeing down some rapids. Your love of something different will dictate your taste, and you are able to pack a lot of activity into a spare day, so early starts are not difficult for you. If you've never done something, you will almost certainly find a way to put it high on your wish list – and if it's slightly dangerous, well, fine!

A **1** man will take on a hobby for a dare. If you are challenged to learn to fly a plane or spend a week at art school, you'll give it a go – and probably come out well for it. Every new activity has the capacity to feed your adrenaline, and, let's face it, **1**s of both sexes are addicted to adrenaline outbursts. Add to this the potential of an audience being open-mouthed at what you are doing, and you have all the ingredients for pleasure. It is just what you like if you can perform for a crowd, explore new territory, and be physically daring all in one serve!

Travel also suits you for leisure time, because it offers fresh places and new faces, but perhaps a city break might entertain you more than a week at a resort – unless the resort can give you water-skiing or skydiving, which would be perfect. In fact, travel is often in your diary as part of your working life too, because you are always pushing to spread new ideas to other people in different places. When it comes to 'where' and 'how', though, you are hard to predict. Most **1** men prefer modern places and ideas to old, so charming historic towns are not really your thing – unless they have been sympathetically brought into the modern era. Thus the New World (both west and east) has a strong appeal for you, especially cities like New York and Sydney, which bustle with energy. But remember that quietude is sometimes appealing for granting that personal space, and when this need kicks in you are probably heading for a week camping in the Rockies. But it would be safe to bet: 'rarely the same place twice'.

Building quite attracts you. Quality leisure hours might be invested in becoming really creative at DIY and learning how to construct more complicated structures. The thrill is, again, in the nature of both the inventive idea and the challenge: if you are ever told you can't do anything, the stubborn side of your nature will prove at all costs that you can.

The explorer in your personality also likes to show how well it can devise new ways of trying old pursuits. This means you are good at orienteering, walking, cycling and climbing – and the side of you that enjoys good food and stimulating company will find a new bar or pub to check out even in familiar places. You also have a nose – of course! – for finding somewhere to sit where no one else is likely to go, or for discovering an unknown gem and getting in way before everyone else gets in on the act!

Oddly enough, perhaps, a **1** man's hobbies are often related to developing a new business interest. Many **1**s – of both sexes – will spend their free time investigating new career pursuits or making money at a second-string interest. You love to improve on existing methods, so even with a well-subscribed sport or artistic talent you will think up new ways of playing with the tools or the toys. Your home life and weekends are rarely dull!

1 IN LOVE

Love: it's what we all want to know about. What's your style as a lover? And your taste – where does that run? Do you want a partner who is, ideally, as independent as you? Or would you rather have a love in your life who is happy to give you the lead and watch patiently while you make your own discoveries? Everything about you screams 'self-confident loner', but is this all there is to your love life?

Our first task is to consider how you see others as potential partners, and what you are likely to need from them. Why are you attracted to someone in the first place? This is where we begin ... But then you might like to pass the book across to your other half (if you have one), for the second subject of discussion is: why are *they* attracted to *you*? What does it mean to have a **1** lover?

Telltale traits of the 1 lover

- Unusual, unpredictable, stands out from the crowd
- Witty, with original chat-up lines
- Sometimes exhibits eccentric behaviour
- Watches others for a long time before saying much, then seizes everyone's attention electrically
- Doesn't follow rules or social expectations
- Wears something red?

How do you do?

A 1 IN ATTRACTION

Whether you're a man or woman, fifty-something or student, when it comes to attraction you know exactly what you want. You have a knack of scanning the largest space and fixing on one other human being who has something *different* about them, some essential quality which intrigues you. It may not be the individual who is universally admired as the most beautiful or striking in the room; neither may it be someone who is without a partner, and thus altogether available. You can identify at fifty paces, though, the most fascinating soul in a gathering.

Being gregarious yourself, you are drawn to a prospective love who is quietly powerful, deeply aware, but not over-talkative. The person who is exuding unhurried charm and grace, and a calm sense of their own dignity, is the one you want to know better. Your ideal love will be someone who is blessed with lots of personality and considerable aesthetic attributes. But most of all, you are unable to get excited about anyone – whatever other merits they boast – who is in any sense dull or predictable.

If at first you don't succeed ...

Needing a challenge in love as well as life, you can't help chasing someone who's hard to get, for whatever reason. And, if you are gently repelled at first go, this will make the second attempt all the more important; 'quit' isn't in your vocabulary.

Once you have made the initial conquest – for persuasiveness is bound to help you do so – your seduction style is going to surprise your quarry. While many **1**s exude nonchalant charm and apparent self-confidence, this is often a deception and belies the insecurities that lurk beneath the surface of the self-reliant persona you broadcast to the world. A quirky sense of humour, however, is such an asset that you often give yourself time to move things on by expressing unusual ideas in a unique way. Plus – and this is a definite draw-card for most – you engineer breathtakingly different dates and invitations out. No one can ever guess what might be on your mind, or where a romantic dinner for two may take them with you in the driving seat. Sunset on a ferry boat or sunrise on the roof of a modern high-rise building are equally possible, and you will always keep one step ahead of your bemused companion.

This will remain true right up to the golden wedding anniversary, if you are genuinely in love. So, for almost anyone who takes the trouble to get close enough to you to know you better, this element of surprise and adventure will be a delight, and will keep things fresh in the relationship for a long time.

Having captured your would-be love's attention, you have a physical ardour and inventiveness that has all the ingredients to please. Clever as you can be with words, you know exactly when to let actions take over, and you may sweep a string of admirers off their feet. Be careful not to bite off more than you can chew in this regard, however, as your push to be entertaining and vigorous would be counted by almost anyone as very serious interest. If you are only getting to know a person and have not yet decided where you want it all to lead, take care not to give them the wrong idea.

Supporting role

Love and affection are important to you in a mate. Even though you are so able to stand up for yourself and be independent, you will expect a partner to support and aid you in the plans you make and the dreams you want to translate into realities. You are heading to the pinnacle in whichever area you have chosen to channel your energies, so you need a very intuitive domestic partner who will allow you to do your own thing and not feel ignored when your focus seems to be elsewhere. This suggests that a high element of trust must exist between you both, and your lover will be more resilient – and have a longevity in your heart – if they, too, can stand on their own at times.

Oh, and respect – did I mention that? You could never love someone who does not command your respect. So, if that gives any mortal being hope that they can fulfil all these executive qualities, perhaps it's time to hand them this book, so they can see what they've let themselves in for ...

To have and to hold?

LOVING A NUMBER 1

If your partner is born under this strongly independent number, they will stretch your sense of self-confidence and also demand that you acquire great intuitive skills, to read between the lines of what they *really* want and what they *say* they want. **1**s never admit how desperately they need approval and affection from those closest to them, and often give the unintentional impression that they are totally self-regulating and jealous of their privacy. Well, self-sufficiency is partly true, but no **1** is the island they seem! This means you need to see beyond the wrapping, understanding, in fact, that there is a very small child inside every **1**, male or female, and that this person needs lots of cuddles and gentle signs of your encouragement in all things.

On the more obvious side, you've clearly been attracted to a very original and perhaps flamboyant soul. Your **1** love is wonderfully charismatic, someone who truly shines in a crowd. If you're honest, that enigmatic, self-determined personality is part of what pulls you; you must be someone who is drawn to people who are individual, and you probably quite like a challenge in love relationships anyway – otherwise you'd never have got yourself into a love affair with a **1**!

This outspoken, creative person will never make you complacent. You are sure to be enjoying an unusual courtship, even well into your old age, forever doing things other people have never tried. Your floor is another person's ceiling: what you find the norm, others would think the exception. You celebrate your private time together when you are a band of just two – company never being requisite to your shared happiness. But then your **1** love has such a magnetic personality that many friends will almost certainly gravitate towards you both, so privacy can be hard to come by.

Why do you love this sometimes wilful and occasionally eccentric person? Easy: a **1** has so many intelligent and different perspectives to offer you on life, and loves to try out new things. This goes beyond the promise that your sex life will keep surprising you. Their wardrobe is full of one-offs (budget permitting), and perhaps may contain individualistic vintage garments from virtually any period. Don't moan about the expense, because one of the things you probably love is that your **1** never dresses the same way as other people. Socially, and at play, they will assume control of most situations (even when you don't always want them to), and their personal image is crucial to what they do. Be sensitive to this when you are forming a critical statement: couch your words tremendously carefully, for **1**s hate criticism and take it *very* personally.

The good, the bad and the ...

Have you got the impression of someone with a fragile (but strong) ego? This is certainly true, and your **1** love is also wilful and impulsive. Seen positively, this means that indecision (which restaurant, holiday venue, house to buy ...) is rarely a problem, for **1**s know what they want and grab it immediately – relegating issues of common sense or affordability to the rear! On the negative side, it may grate when you feel your partner knows it all, and never really acknowledges the part you play. Or, worse, you're not quite sure you're even needed: your **1** is so private and emotionally guarded, with such a dislike of restraint of any kind, that you feel insecure and uncertain of where the relationship is going.

Remember that loving this natural leader, this true character who has so much assertiveness, is not for the faint-hearted. Develop tactful means of phrasing your requests, don't give in to frustrated tempers, and try to diffuse tense situations with humour – for meeting a **1** confrontationally, head-on, will be explosive and probably not very productive! If your **1** is simply too selfish and uncaring, don't be hopeful that this is going to change. But if you can manage the sometimes lonely path, or wondering what to expect next, you'll be rewarded with a lover who has an exciting intellect, a brilliant imagination and a pioneer's enthusiasm for new possibilities, and who will share extraordinary, original observations with you. You'll be much envied by most of your friends, and something unexpected will happen all the time ...

1 in love

Turn-ons:

- ♥✔ A sexy partner who is attractive and a good listener
- ♥✔ Someone who likes strange location-shoots for the love movie you act in together
- ♥✔ A person with a sense of humour and a warm laugh
- ♥✔ Someone who is patient, and not at all like your mother or father!

Turn-offs:

- ♥✗ A demanding partner who asks too many questions or slows you down
- ♥✗ Someone who is cynical or too practical about your dreams
- ♥✗ A lover who must have a shower first thing every morning, no matter where you are
- ♥✗ Anyone who disapproves of you in front of others

1'S COMPATIBILITY

In this weighty section you have the tools to find out how well you click with all the other numbers in matters of the heart, but also when you have to work or play together too. Each category opens with a star-ratings chart, showing you – at a glance – whether you're going to encounter plain sailing or stormy waters in any given relationship. First up is love: if your number matches up especially well with the person you're with, you will appreciate why certain facets of your bond just seem to slot together easily.

But, of course, we're not always attracted to the people who make the easiest relationships for us, and if you find that the one you love rates only one or two stars, don't give in! Challenges are often the 'meat' of a love affair – and all difficulties are somewhat soothed if you both share a birthday number in common, even if that number is derived from the *total* of the birth date rather than the actual **DAY** number. In other words, if your partner's **LIFE** number is the same as your **DAY** number, you will feel a pull towards each other which is very strong, even if the **DAY** numbers taken together have some wrinkles in their match-up. You will read more about this in the pages that follow the star chart.

The charts also include the master numbers **11** and **22**: these bring an extra dimension to relationships for those whose birth-number calculations feature either of these numbers at any stage. (For example, someone with a **DAY** number of **2** may be born on the 29th: 2+9 = **11**, and 1+1 = **2**. This means you should read the compatibility pairings for your number with both a **2** and an **11**.)

Sometimes the tensions that come to the surface in

love relationships are excellent for business relationships instead: the competitiveness that can undermine personal ties can accelerate effectiveness in working situations. We'll take a look at how other numbers match up with yours in vocational situations. And, when it comes to friends, you'll see why not all of your friendships are necessarily a smooth ride ...

In all matters – whether love, work or friendship – you will probably discover that the best partnerships you make involve an overlap of at least one number that you share in common. A number **1** attracts other number **1**s in various close ties throughout life.

NOTE: To satisfy your curiosity, ALL numbers are included in the star charts, so that you can check the compatibility ratings between your friends, co-workers and loved ones – and see why some relationships may be more turbulent than others!

Love

YOUR **LOVE** COMPATIBILITY CHART

	1	2	3	4	5
With a 1	★★★★	★★★★★	★★	★★★	★★★★★
With a 2	★★★★★	★★★★	★★★	★★★★★	★
With a 3	★★	★★★	★★★★★	★★	★★★★
With a 4	★★★	★★★★★	★★	★★★★	★★
With a 5	★★★★★	★	★★★★	★★	★★★
With a 6	★★★	★★★★	★★★★	★★★	★★
With a 7	★★★★★	★★	★★★	★★★★★	★★★
With an 8	★★★★	★★★★	★★★★★	★★★	★★★
With a 9	★★★	★★★	★★★★★	★★	★★★
With an 11	★★★★	★★★★	★★	★★★★★	★★
With a 22	★★★★	★★★★★	★★★	★★★★	★★★★

6	7	8	9	11	22
★★★	★★★★★	★★★★	★★★	★★★★	★★★★
★★★★	★★	★★★★	★★★	★★★★	★★★★★
★★★★	★★★	★★★★★	★★★★★	★★	★★★
★★★	★★★★★	★★★	★★	★★★★★	★★★★
★★	★★★	★★★	★★★	★★	★★★★
★★★★★	★	★★★	★★★★★	★★★★	★★★★
★	★★★	★★★★	★★★	★★★★	★★★★★
★★★	★★★★	★★★	★★	★★★★★	★★★★
★★★★★	★★★	★★	★★★	★★★★	★★★
★★★★	★★★★	★★★★★	★★★★	★★	★★★★★
★★★★	★★★★★	★★★★	★★★	★★★★★	★★

9 8 7 6 5 4 3 2 1

1 in love with a 1 ★★★★

You have a number in common, which already speaks volumes about how you relate to each other. You are a forceful pair of individuals who understand each other's weaknesses and fragilities better than anyone else can. Your taste is probably similar, and you respect the same standards, concepts and ideas. You both value original thinking and are prepared to stand up for what you think is important in this world, so your pursuits are mutual. You want to cover a lot of things in your lifetime, and even when the heat is on – as it often will be – you drive each other to greater and greater feats of activity and achievement. You are doers. Simple as that.

Both of you are born leaders, and yoked together this strength of character gives you a cutting edge over other people. As long as your goals are shared, you can definitely achieve what you want from life. You may even decide to work together and share a business – though you should assign dominion of different spheres to each partner and avoid competing in the same space! Others see you both as a dynamic, trendsetting couple: you will walk into a room and cut a swathe. It helps that you can read each other's minds instinctively, and that you most likely want the same things.

Perhaps what is most attractive about two **1**s being together is that you each feel attraction and appreciation for the other's individuality and independent character. You both know what it takes to stand alone at times against the main body of accepted opinion, and you can support each other through the traumas of this. The possibility of you teaming up to defeat outside competition is excellent.

But there are problems, even with this mostly wonderful pairing. Each of you has a tendency to want to lead and want to speak, more than to be led or be spoken to; and, of course, in every good relationship there are times when one person has to listen to the other, and be acquiescent to their needs and feelings and plans. It will take some work, therefore, to find a harmonious way of sharing the limelight with each other, or sharing the dominant role. It will be better if you can agree to take this in turns, so that one is in charge of some aspects of your co-existence and the other takes on a second set of obligations. If you are both aggressive at the same time, there will be a lot of noise and not much progress over problems.

The challenge for a pair of **1**s falling in love will be to prioritize the co-operative aspects of the relationship, to understand that working individually functions well, as long as you respect each other's need for absolute autonomy at any given time. If you both work independently and empathize with the other partner's need to have this personal freedom, it should be a very good match. You are obviously drawn to one another – the original, energetic, sexy, spirited people that you are! But recognize that a long-lasting relationship demands something special, and that you may have to work at the task of completing what you start together.

Key themes

Strongly physical relationship • Keep a very clean house • Attracted to each other's self-confidence • Able to be 'private' together • Lots of goals reached over time

1 in love with a 2 ★★★★★

You two are naturally drawn to each other, because **1** is a leader and **2** is always ready to follow what is interesting and seems right. As a **1** you have a true appreciation for the aesthetic beauty your **2** exudes, and you will love the gentle and pretty domestic environment **2** is able to provide for you. In fact, **2** offers peace, which is often a real respite from the battles you take on in the big wide world, and this haven also gives you the necessary breathing space to think up clever ideas and 'create' on a large scale.

Most importantly, **2** believes in you. They know you have great plans, and that you're heading somewhere, and, while you are impatient and in a rush to get on, **2** is less frantic and finds a way to help you execute your original ideas. Your sensitive and highly intuitive **2** recognizes your talents and has pride in them. Your leadership qualities are very different from **2**'s wish to shore up their partner's insecurities, and to be the unsung hero. Your **2** has the tact and discretion to smooth over the ruffled feathers you sometimes create by being over-enthusiastic or irritated by conservative thinking. **2** knows you are right, but has the political acumen to put things to the other concerned parties. Your **2** understands instinctively how to support your talents and make sure they come before the right audience.

Being utterly feminine and completely charming – even if he is the male partner! – your **2** brings out the male energy and determination in your number **1** better than anybody else. Where you are innovative, **2** follows through for you; and when you have the need for privacy, **2** is unoffended and helps to create that space for you, defending you even against your own family. **2** knows your bark is usually worse than your bite, even if others are not so sure!

A **1** loving a **2** is one of the best pairings in numerology, because these numbers fit together like night and day. Perhaps no one else will give you as much faith and put as much energy into your dreams as **2** will; and, possibly, no one inspires a **2** more than you can. But there is a difficulty. Sometimes **2**s give the impression of being so compliant that they are weak, and this is not so. **2**s can be stubborn and easily offended, so it is well to remember that the words you say will bruise if they are cruel, and really leave a mark on the gentle **2**, whereas other numbers will know not to pay too close attention – or perhaps have a higher view of themselves. **2** is so willing to give you the lead that you may abuse this at times, and fail to notice their contribution to your success. You shine because, partly, **2** helps you; and you must really fight not to dominate this surprisingly strong and sensitive soul.

Try to be aware that **2** has a lot of the qualities you lack yourself – of being conscious of how others are feeling, of knowing when to back off for a while, of being happy not to be in the forefront. Your **2** can hug you without you asking, because they know – without being told – that you need it. And you have the dynamism and spirit to lift a **2** out of a commonplace or lacklustre life; **2** is not pushy, and often settles for less than perfection just for the sake of tranquillity. You have what it takes to stand up for your **2** and fight their battles as well as your own.

And no one will sing your praises louder.

Key themes

You beautify the space you live in together • Share strong likes and dislikes • Balance of feminine and masculine energy • Inventive sensual relationship, as **2** is a very giving and generous lover

1 in love with a 3 ★★

In friendship, this connection between the creative juices of the **3** and your originality and spark is very good: you sing to the same tune. But in love, this relationship can be exhausting. You are attracted to the **3**'s energy and charm, and, very often, to their physical good looks – **3**s tend to be one of the best-looking numbers! However, there can be a little competition here, with regard to both of you being important and in the limelight, and **3**'s personal magnetism can be a *bête noire* for you sometimes. You are not so much cut from the same cloth, as cut from equally showy, fine-quality cloth of different kinds!

Certainly, your dishy **3** will never bore you, and what does work is that you both love to pack your lives with action and *doing*. You are creative, love the arts, and keep finding interests that appeal to you both. However, **3** expects to be the star in a very humorous – even childlike – way, which will occasionally irritate you. Also, you find **3**'s inability to focus on any one thing to the exclusion of others really infuriating. When you enter a mindset to achieve something, nothing will distract you until all the notes are composed in your head, as it were, and recorded on the page. Then, admittedly, you will delegate the concerto to someone else's hands – the conductor, who will see it through to performance. **3**, though, has too many opuses on the go, and you will feel that nothing ever moves past the ideas stage.

3s are also very indecisive, which can even be a problem at the outset of the attraction between you. You know what you want and what you like – and you want to get on with it and start exploring your **3**'s nature. But this tantalizing person has a tendency to run hot and cold, and it can be confusing. **3**s are often unable to make up their mind as to what they want. It's this person today, and someone else tomorrow. This is not really fickle, but more that they are truly undecided about what works, and it will drive you mad. It may seem as though your **3** can't be loyal – or be trusted.

If you have another number in common, the more positive aspects of the relationship can shine out. This means that the two of you work in synthesis, one handling one set of needs and the **3** probably doing PR for you, while you get the ball rolling and help **3** to put their energies behind something – effectively making up their mind for them. This can help you both to exude a certain gloss and showbiz glamour about you as a pair. When you combine your talents, the sky is the limit.

Trouble comes when **3** makes even you doubt yourself, or when they inadvertently scatter your attention and your energy. You know that you can be impulsive, and this makes **3** nervous. Worse, though, is when your chatty **3** can't sit still or keep quiet, or allow you private space.

Only you can decide how big a problem this is; but it will cause you some frustrations not infrequently!

Key themes

Excellent hosts • Many friends • Good energies • Variety in life together, but often a retreat into individual selfishness and lack of understanding

1 in love with a 4 ★★★

As long as your **4** is content being told what to do, this partnership probably has a better chance of succeeding than people would think. On the face of it, **4** is so pedantic they might really annoy your creative spirit and stop you in mid-flow with issues about practicality. However, in practice your **4** is just the kind of person to help you achieve your goals, being the hard-worker and one person who will stand up to you about the need for proper foundations and good organization.

4s are very often practical to the exclusion of creative interests – but it is not always so, and if your **4** is one of the creative ones, so much the better. **4**s are clever with their hands, and this often manifests as artistic or musical skill, which will have a magnetic appeal for you. You also appreciate the way your **4** listens to you, taking you seriously when others sometimes don't hear you at all. The problem with this is that it seems to be love based on friendship rather than on passion or powerful attraction. Ask yourself this: are you with your **4** because they are useful to you, or because you simply depend on them? If so, you need to work on the problem of being too self-absorbed and (possibly) selfish to see what your 4 needs.

In day-to-day affairs you will be the decision-maker, for **1** always takes the lead and **4** won't challenge that. What can work very well is that your **4** won't always let you rush into things without thinking it through – restraining your impulsiveness at times, when it may be a good to thing to restrain it! **4** sees dangers you don't see; and, while that is often annoying, it is pragmatic and may be of long-term help.

4s love your originality and sense of destiny about life, for things are rarely so glamorous in a **4**'s life. But they can become dull or over-attached to the past, family and routine, and this will discourage you from the natural drive you have to push forwards and try new things. This becomes more than a mere annoyance if the **4**'s cautious nature blunts your wit and imagination. This will certainly create friction, and getting around this basic personality difference will be very challenging.

On the positive side, however, you have a willing accomplice here who can steady you through storms and windy weather emotionally, and whose thoroughness – though so different from your own explosive bluff – can actually make you a wiser and more productive person. This is why it is good for business (*see also page 188*), and why so many **1** and **4** couples do work together, and often from home.

But be wary of something you may not, at first, see. You and your **4** both have very strong opinions, and your **4** needs security in a relationship. If you don't identify this need, you will always be pulling against each other, because your natural inclination is to keep your emotions to yourself. Your **4** is serious, and needs *you* to be so too.

Key themes

Shared love of family • Comfortable home with material trappings • Need to balance impatience of **1** with extreme patience of **4** • Enjoyment of garden and green places • **1** not to 'order' **4** around

1 in love with a 5 ★★★★★

Fizz! Bang! This relationship pops and crackles. You are extremely drawn to each other physically, and have a need to get out and feel the wind in your faces and the world under your feet. There is a strong magnetism here, which is tangible to all those who see you together. You are not going to sit on your hands, either of you, and this relationship should be able to withstand most problems it encounters, for you work well with one another in almost all areas.

Your **5** is interesting and original, just as you are, and always up for a last-minute dash to some odd place to watch the sun rise. In fact, **5** can't sit in one place for long, and this is one of the few threats to your mutual happiness – because you do like (and need) your solitude at times. How can you draft your new visions if the **5** won't stay still long enough to let you get settled? You will need to work out how to give each other appropriate personal time.

Money will materialize well between you, for both of you have a capacity to think up ideas and work hard to make them realities. Your **5** easily promotes your skills and strengths, and knows how to attract finance for your projects. Difficulty comes when **5** also wants to spend a lot of money – and you may not share this constant love of luxury. However, if you can indulge them sometimes, it may not have to burgeon out of control! And you like many nice things yourself, so you just need to agree a limit.

What you will really enjoy together is a sexy love style which bends the rules that other people seem to need to live by. You both enjoy the physical aspects of your relationship, and things may get very experimental. Suffice to say you are less likely to run out of steam in the bedroom than many relationships! This also means that you may never need – or want – to stray from one another, for you will never settle for the same old thing, or get stuck in a rut. You are both unconventional – the **5** even more than you – and you will find some very romantic, as well as sensual, ways to satisfy each other's curiosity.

You share a respect for education, and it is quite possible that you have several academic interests in common, and that you'll go on learning together for many years. You each have an intelligent mind and a good wit, so stretching yourselves together is a way to continually interest one another and keep things fresh. But your **5** is also given to ups and downs, or feeling the blues, so you will have to be a wise counsellor, as well as a good lover, to this partner. They are restless, and sometimes this footloose-and-fancy-free yearning can be more than even *you* have bargained for. Moreover, your standards are sometimes at odds, so, over the years, you will need to maintain your feeling of originality, and not slip into conventionalism, if your trust of each other is to stay strong.

Help your **5** unwind if you can, offering them tranquillity and forcing some calm on them even when they seem to resist you.

Key themes

5 loves their freedom but **1** recreates a feeling of freshness and individuality daily • Both partners take chances and have a strong sense of daring • A very sexy relationship where each learns how to satisfy the other • Likelihood of earning well together and living with money

1 in love with a 6 ★★★

Oops! This is going to be interesting. You have a relationship that works as an attraction of opposites, in many ways, with your **6** enticing you to slow down and take things carefully, rather than rush off and try to do everything all at once. This is out of care for you rather than an over-cautious nature, though it won't always seem so to you. However, if anyone can get you to admit you need a hug sometimes, maybe this person can. **6** is the number of love, and a **6** is a soul wanting to be loved above all else. Result: they will force you to feel your emotions, ask you for a kiss, and tell you when you are being impossible – but ever so gently!

If you are too self-occupied, your **6** will languish. Every personal pain and hurt your **6** love feels is related to being loved and needed, whereas your wishes are to be left alone to work things through on your own. A **6** is not emotionally weak, but is made strong by love, so you need to be as expressive as possible if you really love this person and want to make it work over time. You will also need to get on with their family – to be prepared to have an extended group of people in your life. Or, if your **6** doesn't have that many family members, this will be a source of some pain to them, so you need to bear this in mind, too.

You love your **6**'s good taste, and you will learn from it. A **6** can get you to look at the world in a different light, and they may also just about persuade you to be more sociable and outgoing than your number is inclined to be. What they will love is the way in which you shine for them and for others, and, if you don't abuse this power, you can be very exciting for a **6**, and open their horizons. However, the seesaw begins to tip the other way if you insist on always seeing things only from your own perspective, and ignoring your gentle **6**'s feelings. Sharing creative tastes and projects will probably be the best way to appreciate each other's artistic streak and allow yourselves to be individuals sharing time and space together.

Clashes will happen. They may centre around your feeling that your **6** is over-protective of other people in your lives; or it may be that your **6** seems to smother you occasionally, without letting you have your own room or friends. Not everything between you will be shared, and your **6**'s tendency to be self-sacrificing may bother you, or even make you angry. Once your respect is lost it is hard to regain. But most of the adjustments must come from you, and it will be imperative that you fight the urge to be dictatorial or pushy just because your **6** seems to take longer than you do to decide on a direction to take or to complete a task.

Be aware that you may fall off the pedestal your **6** wants to put you on. So high are the ideals your **6** wants to find in people, that it is sometimes unrealistic to expect anyone to live up to them. Be gentle, though, in how you bring this to their attention.

Key themes

Shared pride in children and family (if they go on to have one) • **6** has an urge for luxury, and wants a beautiful place to live • **1** excites **6**'s pride in them, but has to give in to much socializing

1 in love with a 7 ★★★★★

This is a marriage of true minds, in a way. You have so many character traits in common that it seems inevitable you will attract each other. Better yet, you attract each other's good qualities! Your **7**'s enigmatic reserve and intelligence are a magnet for you, and you seem to reach into your most spiritual inclinations when you come together with this number.

However, you will need to curb your propensity to say exactly what you think without pausing for thought, because **7**s think very deeply and analytically, and will question your more impulsive reactions. You will risk their wrath if you appear to be brash or crude. Also, if you're too demanding you will lose them: they have a need for keeping some corners of their personality from everybody – even from the love of their life. You are private, too, but even you may feel that there is a well of pain, experience or loneliness which lies behind your **7**'s complex nature, and you may never be allowed to go there. Be patient about this, for it isn't personal. Yet, if you can wait, you may be ultimately rewarded with a confidence. **7**s will speak in their own time.

You are a born extrovert, but your **7** is a little bit introverted – in some departments, at least. Even if your **7** has another more outgoing number as their **LIFE** number, you are still dealing with someone who builds a wall of silence around them. Family memories and early shaping experiences cast a long shadow. A **7** lover needs you to be aware of their depth, their need for truth and honesty, but their desire for independence. Some of these ideas seem contradictory – yet they are all true. If a relationship between you is to work, you will have to cultivate more patience than you usually show, and be a tasteful and generous lover.

One of the qualities you most admire in your **7** is their shrewd brain and their inner poise and dignity: the poise comes, in fact, from a capacity to see into people and into things so profoundly, and with such serenity. They, in turn, admire your sharp mind and originality, for **7**s are in many ways intellectual snobs who can't be bothered with uneducated minds. This will suit you, more often than not. As a pair, you will have a house of books and music, wine and – possibly – antiques. And, although you like many modern things, your **7** shares your taste for one-offs. This can lead to some very interesting journeys together – both metaphysical and actual.

Your physical relationship may be excellent. A **7** lover will have more composure than you, and your energy may at times seem exhausting to them, but this is potentially a very powerful and empathetic relationship. Both of you focus well, and know what you want. Each of you has an attractive amount of self-reliance and individuality which excites the other one. You are both clever loners, and you will find enough to occupy you in one another if you can just give each other an inch here or there.

Do try to meet your **7** halfway on their standards of health and neatness: they will not be happy living in a messy apartment, and function best in an environment that is elegant and precise. In fact, probably the worst problem for you to negotiate is that your **7** is critical of everything and everyone – especially of themselves – and you are sensitive to criticism. Don't let the organization of the space you share together become a matter of contention.

Key themes

Both have very original taste – you generate a stunning home atmosphere • Spur each other's creative concepts • 1 strains against 7's perfectionism • Intelligent conversations • Private time shared between you well

1 in love with an 8 ★★★★

This is a relationship with at least occasional fireworks. You are both aggressive in a positive way, and you like to make things happen, so this allows for the chance of a really dynamic bond with much mental activity and physical pleasure in the offing. Of course, there is also the chance that you may become rivals! It very much depends on whether you are attracted to one another in a narcissistic fashion, or simply admire the qualities you each exude. Co-operation is the key point.

When you harness your considerable mental acuity and drive, you have the kind of combined potential that most businesses would dream of – which is one reason why you are an excellent business team (*see also page 196*). In love, however, you are likely to bring out the best and the worst in each other, because it is of no account which of you is the female and which the male, since both numbers are dominant. You can either decide to join each other, and let your talents work in unison, or destroy each other with too much competitive energy.

Naturally, this electrical kind of attraction – with sparks flying in all directions – is great for sex! Your physical magnetism may be just what got you started, and it will probably go on working well even when other facets of your relationship become rocky. The basic problem is that the **8** wants to take control of your ideas and move them outwards to a broader audience, but, in doing so, you may feel pressured to compromise your own individuality. Also, it may frustrate you that your charismatic **8** tries to do all of the jobs and become all things to all people – leaving no time for you personally. And, there are definitely clashes of ego ahead between you.

But the good bits are very good. You both have diverse interests, speak your mind, and have an intensity about you – especially when it comes to getting projects started. Your **8** is generous and loves seeing you in good humour, full of laughter, so you often bring this out in each other with a touch of eccentricity. You can be quick to anger, each of you, but your **8** gets over it – if you will let them. You have to try to do the same, and not brood for too long on an injury.

Accept that you are both ambitious, and try not to outdo each other by wanting to make a grand entrance wherever you go. Pool your resources and make things really happen around you both. Try to get your fascinating **8** to slow down and make time for love. You are both so intolerant of time-wasters and plodding thinkers that you could easily fly to the moon together, but patience is not a strong point for either of you, so you will have to act out of character with each other at times, if you are to grow together and hear what is hurting inside. The possible rewards will be well worth it.

Key themes

Pair of go-getters who neighbours and friends will struggle to keep up with • Hot-tempered flashes between you • Inclined to over-action and exaggeration • Distinctive home with beautiful material furnishings

9 8 7 6 5 4 3 2 1

1 in love with a 9 ★★★

This love relationship can work particularly well, because you are a starter and your trusty **9** likes to finish things off, if possible: a perfect harmony of wills. And, too, your interesting **9** has such a depth of vision regarding what may be possible that it inspires your best energies and drives you forward with clever ideas. So far, all good. Your originality gets a fine-tuning from your **9**, and you respect this person for being many things that you are not – as do they with you.

The wind blows across the emotional waters between you, however, when you feel as though you are always in the driving seat and working hard to motivate your moody **9**. On a good day, their moods are divine – for it is a spiritual number, full of hope, of looking for what is good in others. But on a down day, how can you motivate this person to feel better about themselves? They go over and over the things that upset them, never letting go of hurts from previous times, and you just want to push forwards and make a new life.

On the credit side, you appreciate each other's very distinctive – and quite different – sense of humour, and you enjoy the sympathy your **9** lover gives you ... the way you are really listened to ... the time they will take to please you ... the warmth and patience they exhibit, which is a balm for your own haste and inner turmoil. You can have fun together, enjoying activities that some might see as childlike. You are both idealistic, and your **9** can fall in love with dramatic depth of feeling, inspiring a loyalty in you that you are longing to give. You like the way others will seek out your lover for advice, to listen, because they are indeed both clever and (usually) wise. And your **9** will be in awe of your single-mindedness and your determined energies.

But if your **9** has had a traumatic start in life – as many do – you will discover that there are two sides to their personality in love. Sometimes your **9** is generous, and shares their thoughts with you, but at other times they withdraw and lapse into self-interest. This number often creates relationships that are odd or strange, with too much inclination to self-sacrifice. This is the least helpful character trait, when teamed with your own propensity to be self-reliant, for it will annoy and confuse you. And, if your **9** wallows for too long on any point, which is always possible, you will lose respect for them, and your love will become strained.

The other critical problem – which may be more noticeable after time – is that your **9** can be too indecisive for your taste. You have worked out when and where you are going, and your **9** may be still vacillating with bags packed and passport in hand. Or, you may find that dragging your sensitive **9** out of dark spaces is not always easy, so you travel or go out alone.

Yet, if your combined energies – your courage, and your **9**'s wisdom – can be directed well, you may be one of the happiest and most attractive couples on the planet. It all hinges on how well you can *push*, without being too pushy!

Key themes

1 will take the lead, but **9** will finish whatever you start together • **9** brings out the artistic side of **1** better than anybody • **1** can help the **9** to discover greater self-confidence • **1** adds a bit of dash and genius to **9**'s real intelligence

1 in love with an 11 ★★★★

Mmm. Very interesting. This is a **2** with the characteristics of a **1** thrown in, as the number is made up of two **1**s that never really reduce back to **2**. You are impressed with the inspirational qualities of this striking lover – someone whom everyone looks up to, or at – and you love the image that you know you create as a couple, when you go out or arrive anywhere. Together, you certainly can make a splash. In fact, your **11** love may be more ambitious and more driven even than you, and loves to find unique ways of doing absolutely anything. So, at one level, you've met your match ...

... Almost! But what will take its toll will be your extraordinary **11**'s ups and downs, highs and lows, which come in equal measure. The moodiness of a **9** partner doesn't compete with the up-swings of an **11**. Here is a number which never stands on one solid piece of ground, for there are always two numbers that underlie the **11**'s energies and interests, and this results in twin personalities beyond anything you can encounter elsewhere (except, partly, with a **22**; *see page 176*). Which, of course, fascinates you, too.

'Challenge' is your favourite word, and you'll be on your toes here with someone whose flair and sparkle attract you both sexually and intellectually. You will learn so much from this partner, and find their unique ways of solving problems completely mesmerizing. You will be drawn to their command of so many disciplines, and won over by their resourcefulness and interest in others. No one motivates other people quite as well as **11**s and, indeed, **22**s. But is this likely to compete too much with your own personality? You like to be the one who gets others on their feet too. You both love to be right, and neither of you gives an inch. Can you resolve this problem, and mine the diamond you could have from the unhewn rock that symbolizes your union?

The answer to this question lies at the heart of the success or failure of the whole relationship with this individual. They will definitely never let you lapse into complacency, keeping you guessing about what they are planning, where they are heading, what they think of you. And nothing is more attractive. If they also exhibit many of the qualities of the implicit number **2**, as well, then you will have a lover who is supportive of you, and who knows how to be co-operative in key situations.

Potential strife comes from the similarity between you, and the fact that you recognize so many traits – both attractive and unattractive – in one another. You bring out the best, but also the worst, in each other. You both want to lead, and are both used to attracting attention and admiration from your followers. If you can agree on which way it is that you want to go, you will build a heaven; but if you antagonize and disorientate one another, you're building more of a hell. This is either a perfect match or a perfect mismatch, and which it is will depend on how you organize your exceptional combined talents and visions.

Key themes

Life in the fast lane • Dash and daring flavour all your pursuits together • Arguments can be fast and furious • Both partners justify their own viewpoint and position • Bound to live somewhere very distinctive

1 in love with a 22 ★★★★

Like an **11**, this soul attracts you powerfully. You know quality when you see it, and this is someone who is a bit special. They are authoritative, calm and yet excitable, unruffled, for the most part. You love their personal style – the cut of their clothes, their quiet awareness of an overall superiority to nearly everyone around them, and yet their surprising lack of apparent ego. This is someone you want to know very well – a lover you want to slow down for, if necessary. This person is going somewhere, and you want to go too.

But your **22** will not be pushed around. You will have to accommodate their thinking on every issue, because – unlike the more compliant **4**, who is happy to let you take the credit for what you mutually achieve – this is someone who needs to be recognized, who will stand up for what is just and right. You have a crusader in your life here, and you will be impressed by all that they do or say, but it is a different method of 'doing' to your own. You will need to discover how generous you can be, if this is to work really well. Which it may.

Together, you have the potential to create a very good income together. Your **22** is one of life's 'master draughtsmen', and you love to recognize an opportunity and then make it happen. You both have great personal determination and resources of talent, and you are each highly original – though perhaps in different ways. Your **22** love is a law unto themselves, finding moral integrity and courage in their own unusual view of the world, while your originality is in seeing extraordinary possibilities in ordinary starting points. Working as a team, though, you can discover solutions to problems that mystify others. This augurs well for love, but also for business relationships, and you may decide to go into business together (*see also page 202*).

One thing that can be a problem is that your **22** lives off quite a bit of nervous energy (unlike a **4**), and likes to work right through any project until it's done. This can mean long hours, travel commitments, late nights. At best, this gives you that valuable time-alone space that you crave, but it also means you can, occasionally, drift apart. And, overwork for both of you can bring on emotional stresses.

Perhaps the hardest aspect of this mainly excellent pairing is the way in which your **22** clings to strong opinions that are borne of much wisdom. Your own views are equally strong, and, as with **11**, competitiveness between you can be an unexpected drama. You love one-offs in every arena, whether it be fashion, your home or your work platform – and you will certainly have a one-off in a relationship with this person. You need to decide whether your energies will feel sufficiently expressed if you give much of yourself to helping your **22** achieve their destiny.

It is not in the nature of **1** to be a second fiddle to anyone, and yet a **22** needs someone to support them when they are headed right up the pole – professionally, politically, or whatever it is they are doing. Are you willing?

Key themes

Headed somewhere glamorous together • Pair of highly capable individuals • **22** doesn't let **1** have it all their own way • **1** is sometimes talking to the wall when **22** is thinking • Both of you have a wonderful wardrobe!

Work

YOUR WORK COMPATIBILITY CHART

	1	2	3	4	5
With a 1	★★★★	★★★★★	★	★★★	★★★
With a 2	★★★★★	★★★	★★★	★★★★	★
With a 3	★	★★★	★★★★	★★	★★★★★
With a 4	★★★	★★★★	★★	★★★★★	★★★
With a 5	★★★	★	★★★★★	★★★	★★
With a 6	★★	★★★★★	★★★★	★★★★	★★★★
With a 7	★★★★★	★★★	★★★	★★★★★	★★
With an 8	★★★★★	★★★★★	★★★★★	★★★	★★★★
With a 9	★★★★	★★★	★★★★★	★★	★★★
With an 11	★★	★★★★	★★★	★★★★★	★★
With a 22	★★★★★	★★	★★★	★★★	★★★★

6	7	8	9	11	22
★★	★★★★★	★★★★★	★★★★	★★	★★★★★
★★★★★	★★★	★★★★★	★★★	★★★★	★★
★★★★	★★★	★★★★★	★★★★★	★★★	★★★
★★★★	★★★★★	★★★	★★	★★★★★	★★★
★★★★	★★	★★★★	★★★	★★	★★★★
★★★	★	★★★★	★★★	★★★★★	★★★★
★	★★★★	★★★	★★	★★★★	★★★★★
★★★★	★★★	★★★	★★★★	★★★★★	★★★★
★★★	★★	★★★★	★★★	★★★★★	★★★★★
★★★★★	★★★★	★★★★★	★★★★★	★★★★	★★★★★
★★★★	★★★★★	★★★★	★★★★★	★★★★★	★★★

9 8 7 6 5 4 3 2 1

1 working with a 1 ★★★★

1 and **1** makes **2**, an enviable team. Of course, you need to assign each other different spheres for expression, so that you each have domain over what interests you best. The usual outcome of two **1**s in business is of an energetic, 'go-get-'em' kind of establishment that breaks all the conventional rules about what went before, and finds new dimensions for the field you're in together. You excite and drive each other, and understand one another's motives brilliantly.

Sometimes it may seem as though it's the two of you against the world, with others looking on, amused at the projects you dream up or the ideas you feel entitled to experiment with. And often you will do something very different, out of the ordinary, involving strange hours or places, and having to travel down some lonely roads. Not everyone will approve. But most will admit you've done something with your time, and had fun along the way.

Difficulties can arise – primarily, if you both want to be 'chief', without any willing followers or co-workers. If you pull against each other, everyone else will duck for cover. And temper tantrums? Quite possible. But an establishment with two **1**s in close proximity is usually bright and airy and full of excitement. You will make more than enough money if you concentrate on it, although temptations just to 'try things out' because no one else has may arise – without regard to whether it's good business sense. So be it. There are more things to life.

Key themes

Feisty • Lively • Different • Unusual business ideas • Strange hours

1 working with a 2 ★★★★★

This is the co-worker you've been longing for. Diplomatic **2** understands just what is required before you've asked, bringing you tea or organizing lunch: this is a five-star working relationship. This assessment *does* work on the assumption that **1** is giving the orders. If the **2** is telling *you* what to do, big ego adjustments may be needed – and, in fact, **2** would rather be the quieter partner, as well. But the energy you manage to generate together is highly effective, and there will also be a feeling of harmony in the environment you work in together. In short, **2** keeps you calm.

Occasionally, you feel your **2** co-worker is a doormat, or you forget to say 'thank you' when they fill their usual role of seeing to your needs. This word is easy to overlook, because **2** never seems to ask for it, but if you never say it you are ruining a good relationship. A **2** at work is gentle and efficient but not weak, so remember your manners!

2 always looks on **1**'s creativity with appreciation, and admires your ambition and focus; **2**s can also often ignore your aggressive streak, because they understand that it can be positive, and have a desirable outcome. Don't say unkind things, though, or tease them. **2** functions smoothly at work, supports everyone, gets on with most people, but doesn't give in on the odd occasion they reach their own conclusion, even if it differs from yours. Just sometimes, be prepared to give in gracefully. Trust **2**'s intuition: if they do dig their heels in, they'll have a good reason.

Key themes

Smooth running • Calm space • Efficient • Good understanding

1 working with a 3 ★

You like **3**'s creativity, but not their lack of organization. If left to a **3**, no decision would be reached, which is precisely the opposite to what you want to do – and quickly! It could be argued that you have the willpower to make **3** settle on one front, but at work this is a poor formula for success. Your **3** co-worker gets on with everyone, and it chafes that even the tea break turns into a party around them. **3**s feel there's always time to listen to someone's tale.

3 isn't lazy, or unwilling to do a job. On the contrary: they will try their hand at many things, being creative and amenable in all of them. **3** is also prepared to stay back, to be flexible about what they're asked; but you're happier knowing an expert is in charge of their post. Something about **3**'s dilettantism drives you to despair. You are both artistic, have flair, exude energy, wit and charm. **3**, though, transmits nervous energy, which makes *you* nervous, and is not keen on your perceived tactlessness. You speak directly if something needs articulating, but **3** shivers if you are brutal to weaker people. **3** weaves circles to make a difficult point; you have different methods – even if you ultimately come to the same conclusion. **3** is genuinely talented, and has a way with things – but it's just not *your* way.

On a good day, a **3** will amuse you and make you laugh when deadlines are too close or pressures mount. This is what **3** *can* do for you. But, in other respects, you are two talented souls who brush each other up the wrong way, so if you are working together put some space between you and mind your tongues!

Key themes

Unpredictable • Volatile • Disorganized • Baffling ... but creative

1 working with a 4 ★★★

A curate's egg, this working relationship is good in parts. You can induce the **4** to really utilize their powers of concentration and dedication, because they believe in you. And you recognize a vital team-player when you see one – someone whose own ego is unimportant in the scheme of things, but who appreciates the importance of where you are taking everyone. You have a different approach, but it's an approach that works productively.

4s have a great deal of skill in a number of areas, and you are perhaps one of the first people who has thanked them for that. You are aware of how much they add, of how their practical and logical assessment of what is required to achieve any task is vital, if it is to move from planning board to existence. **4** looks at the cost, the time needed, the materials involved, and analyses this for you so that you are free to create and imagine new pastures. And, together, you can talk the doubters down because, if reliable **4** gets behind you, no one else can have anything to say. If you can make a **4** see things your way, then anyone can.

The going gets rough when you feel the **4**'s excessive practicality gets in the way of making plans, for your **4** team-mate has a knack for finding problems and raising objections, simply as a matter of gathering all the details. Your imagination will already have taken your company to the top of its niche (worldwide!) while the **4** is still working out how to pay the rent! The **4** does have faith in you, however, and – provided you don't have to live together – you should make a very productive business team. Just give them time – *always* – to mull over the ideas.

Key themes

Well-balanced skills • Seen as the 'odd couple'

1 working with a 5 ★★★

In an office environment, **1** and **5** can be a surprise package. The **5** is an exuberant, sometimes boundless, enthusiast for almost any original idea, which means you have someone who has already decided your concepts are good before you've even voiced them. The worry is that no one's looking at the fine print – so it would help if a **2** or a **4** is available for that! After all, if you two get going, who will stop you?

5 is a born promoter – the proverbial salesman who can take oil to Texas – and you are the one who comes up with the ideas worth selling. You devise it; they verbalize it. Together, you generate lively discussions and clever approaches to work, and others find you both good company and utterly positive in what you do. Moreover, you are lucky together, and give each other a boost when people around you seem flat and uninspired.

The light flashes amber when you both need the approval of a crowd, or when **5** feels you're taking too much merit for an achievement. **5** is happy with others taking their part, and may be irritated by your wish for privacy and seclusion in order to develop strategies for business. Why not talk them through? The other problem for a **5** is in accomplishing routine work, or anything demanding a long stint at one thing, or in one place. This suggests that you need others to fill in crucial links for both of you – others in the team who will soften the dynamic between two boisterous, confident people. But the pairing of a **5** and a **1** at work is clever, and you should be able to inspire each other to greater heights and fresher ideas over time.

Key themes

Zinging atmosphere • Several balls in the air • Good contact • Others required for back-up

1 working with a 6 ★★

You are a person who wants to make things happen, and this will have one of two possible effects on a **6** in business. Either you may inspire the **6** to believe in their artistic talents and people skills so much that you galvanize them into action, rather than letting them hide behind other more extroverted people; or, you may eclipse them into permanent retirement and depression. **6** is sensitive, at home and at work, and needs gentle handling. The result of taking the trouble to do this is that you have a really diligent worker who has much to contribute, because they feel so strongly for others. There will be times, though, when you feel they are too soft, or wasting their hours on unworthy causes!

When you have a brilliant idea, it is a **6** who can teach that idea – or its uses – to others. The **6** has the diplomacy you often lack, and is willing to take time coaxing people. But your energy levels are quite different. You prefer to blazon your way through obstacle courses, while the **6** is opposed to harsh or blustering methods. Sometimes you will have to accept that you see things differently.

Businesses that would feed off the abilities you share are products or services which demand original ideas but offer beauty or comfort for the home, or are related to fashion or food. Here your energies pair up well, and you will discover a mutual respect for each other. You will admire **6**'s taste and often give them precedence in work decisions which need an aesthetic element to succeed.

Key themes

Can please many parties • Draw inspiration from each other • Marry different types of expression

1 working with a 7 ★★★★★

You two make a very positive pairing in business. You are both full of inner strength, and like to do things brilliantly, never settling for second best. In fact, **7** can perfect what you start, and you are able to retire to opposite sides of a room and get on with it, without interference. The **7** may have the specialist education you admire, but you have the raw ability and daring that they may feel they lack. Your fearlessness combined with **7**'s discipline could move financial mountains, so suffice to say you're a good team.

Your working options together are unlimited, because **7** is brilliant at research and you are a pioneer/explorer type. You will find interesting ways of looking at problems, and spur each other to solve them together; but while you can be something of a jack of all trades, the **7** likes to specialize – which you value. You ask a question, and **7** will know how and where to find the answer.

You're both quick on the uptake, and neither of you needs another person to agree with what you envisage. You are replete as a band of two, and many new frontiers at work have been achieved through this kind of partnership. You would be happiest in your own shared business, rather than working for a corporation, but as long as you have a degree of autonomy you will succeed very well together at almost anything you try. You'll be especially in your element if you can find a work environment that offers rural tranquillity – even if it's in the city – or if the building you occupy is unusual. In an ideal world, **1** and **7** will gravitate towards water, or a park, for an office location!

Key themes

Well suited for team work • Good grasp of one another's strengths • Respect for each other's minds

1 working with an 8 ★★★★★

The very idea of this pairing spells 'big business'. Here are a couple of potential moguls, and if you are both languishing in a corner doing unspectacular things you are underselling your capabilities and under-achieving. Perhaps no one has more natural talent for business than you two, but you need distinct roles to avoid a strong clash of wills!

If you're looking for an inspired partner to form a business with, look no further. An **8** thinks on the grand scale, which you will love – for no obstacles are really an impediment to success for the two of you. Just like you, **8** likes to have more than one project on the go, and if you are given charge of a business which is failing, or limping along, the two of you can move it to unsuspected heights. **8** never relies on luck, but finds out exactly what is needed and provides it. Usually well-educated (even if self-taught), an **8** is ready to see potential in what you are imagining, and to help you get your concept out there. If a new project of your design requires a crash course in some new field, or a mastery of any previously untried discipline, **8** will find the means to do it. No one can see your visions as clearly, or understand better how to set you ticking until you find a way to change the existing landscape. **8** appreciates you.

Emergency situations will somehow frequently arise around the two of you, because you push each other – and everyone else – to the top of their game. Be warned not to run yourselves ragged in pursuit of perfection, and allow each other the freedom of your own patch, so you don't thwart each other's intentions.

Key themes

Excellent for sparking off each other • Complementary skills • Generate humour and largesse with colleagues

1 working with a 9 ★★★★

This is another pair of well-met souls at the office. You have the kind of forcefulness and optimism that helps 9 get out of bed on a stressful day, and they have the overall clarity to see how to make your business ideas turn into actualities. You start well, and the **9** finishes for you once you lose interest! Best of all, you create a feeling of goodness in the people who work around you, for **9**s keep you in high spirits, while you stop **9**s from worrying overly. And what good ideas you come up with together!

You have a way of knowing exactly what the **9** has to offer – perhaps a better sense than they do. Time and again you will pick out the one diamond from the bag of crystals which pours metaphorically from **9**'s creative imagination; but, equally, **9** can put your feelings into words for others. **9** will mimic you, but you'll see the funny side; no other number tends to get away with as much around you as they do. You also both share a flair for the dramatic, and you'll have fun teaming up for any promotional work or public relations exercises that come into your business's needs.

You have the talent to produce something original, which **9** can, in turn, make useful as well. All **9**s like to be of service to other people, and neither of you will be happy if confined to menial tasks, so together you are likely to break out of the humdrum, and create excitement around you. And if ever someone has to plead your case for you, to another audience or critic, **9** can do it. They just *get* how you do things, and are inclined to play along with even your maddest schemes!

Key themes

Rally each other's spirits • Starter teamed with finisher • Intuit one another's best gifts for work

1 working with an 11 ★★

An interruption to the flow of great business pairings here: you are too much alike, in the worst possible ways, to do well sharing a career. You both want to be the star player, have a fragile ego, and need a string of seconds to do your bidding. You each know what makes the other tick, and don't trust each other because you could both do what the other is doing. If anything, the **11** makes you feel stupid at times, while you make them feel fragmented. To you, the **11** is unstable; to them, you're a bit rough around the edges. In a nutshell, you don't bring out the best in one another.

If you are truly evolved souls, and have got past the competitive stage, you may be able to appreciate that you are both dynamic risk-takers with great personal courage and the capacity to work tirelessly for extended periods. Perhaps the **11** is a little too metaphysical for your taste, seeming to have their intelligent head in the clouds sometimes, while you'd rather have yours intent on the horizon, looking for what lies just ahead. At work, the **11** relies on intuition more than you do – the difference being that your instincts are based on sound, lightning-fast assessments of what you see, whereas the **11** sees what is not in the least expressed. But you are both highly creative and genuinely inventive, so it's a pity you can't put your differences aside more often and help each other across the finishing line.

Best opportunities for doing well together are in the teaching professions, as both of you can be inspirational. Competing in straight business, though, may be very trying for those around you.

Key themes

Similar to point of friction • Two stars who want equal billing • Extraordinary potential that seems to go awry

9 8 7 6 5 4 3 2 1

1 working with a 22 ★★★★★

This is someone most people work well with, because they take the abilities of a **4** and make something more exciting from them. For you, working with a **22** is a privilege. They will rely on your powers to stir up whatever is inert and old-fashioned and push across the frontier into new pastures of hope. If you work with a **22**, you will be given scope to do anything and everything you can to make use of your energies and talents for the good of many people. They may be able to prevent you from offending others, too, because they understand your best talents are in design rather than negotiation – unless everyone is asleep, in which case **22** will send you in to wake them up!

You have a mutual understanding of what excites one another. You realize the **22** is different, a deep thinker wanting to create a fairer world; they, in turn, realize you have the drive and bravery to argue for that world's existence. You are the new blood **22** needs to execute their wishes. Together, you have very high ideals and know how to take a practical suggestion and make it nationally appealing.

You will know there is more to your **22** colleague, arguing for circumspection from others about the way they seem to do things. You recognize talent, and understand that people who are different are so for a reason. If no one stood out from the crowd, things would stay the same – and this would frustrate both of you. And, when you feel you have discovered something new and extraordinary, your powerful ally will champion your cause. Overall, this is a very positive, and potentially constructive, work bond.

Key themes

Instinctive mutual appreciation • Shared directives • Very physical approach to getting things done

Friendship

YOUR **FRIENDSHIP** COMPATIBILITY CHART

	1	2	3	4	5
With a 1	★★★	★★★★★	★★	★★★	★★★
With a 2	★★★★★	★★	★★★	★★★★	★
With a 3	★★	★★★	★★★★	★	★★★★
With a 4	★★★	★★★★	★	★★★★★	★★
With a 5	★★★	★	★★★★	★★	★★★
With a 6	★	★★★★	★★★★★	★★★	★★★★
With a 7	★★★★	★★★★★	★★★★	★★★★★	★
With an 8	★★★★	★★★★	★★★★★	★★	★★★★
With a 9	★★★★	★★★	★★★★	★★★★	★★★★
With an 11	★★★	★★★★★	★★	★★★★★	★★
With a 22	★★★	★★★	★★★★	★★	★★★

6	7	8	9	11	22
★	★★★★	★★★★	★★★★	★★★	★★★
★★★★	★★★★★	★★★★	★★★	★★★★★	★★★
★★★★★	★★★★	★★★★★	★★★★	★★	★★★★
★★★	★★★★★	★★	★★★★	★★★★★	★★
★★★★	★	★★★★	★★★★	★★	★★★
★★★★	★	★★★★	★★★★	★★★	★★★★★
★	★★★★	★★★	★★	★★★★★	★★★★★
★★★★	★★★	★★★★	★★★★	★★★★★	★★★
★★★★	★★	★★★★	★★	★★★★	★★★★
★★★	★★★★★	★★★★★	★★★★	★★★★★	★★★★
★★★★★	★★★★★	★★★	★★★★	★★★★	★★

9 8 7 6 5 4 3 2 1

You get on well with a lot of people, though you will have moments of wanting peace and privacy from every single one of them! Let's see which are the best combinations ... and which are the worst:

1 and **1** (★★★): You have a lot in common, but the friendship has less to offer than either love or business relationships. You tend to compete more as pals – one-upping each other at times – whereas respect in love or work softens this difficulty.

1 and **2** (★★★★★): As with all other relationships, there is a natural pecking order that sees you take the leading role, with the **2** in a – mostly – happy and supporting part. Your **2** friends quietly tell you the truth, and know how to mollify your moods!

1 and **3** (★★): A little too much conflict over the basic necessities of life. Your **3** friends have too much fragmented energy, and wear you out. They can never be still, or go anywhere without their telephone. And they don't think deeply enough, to your mind.

1 and **4** (★★★): These people make good friends to most numbers, and you will find them solid and honest, which you like. They don't inspire you, though, and lack the willingness to do outrageous things with you, so it is a good bond but has limitations for you.

1 and **5** (★★★): You both appreciate the side of each other's personality that offers similarities: energy, humour and a wish to get on with life. Neither of you are passive, but occasionally **5**'s restlessness is too much for you, and you will often fall out.

1 and **6** (★): Your **6** friends have a style and gentleness which you can admire, but it is not your cup of tea. Their lives seem too staid and timorous for you, and they, frankly, find you too self-centred and bombastic to rest for long in their gentle lives.

1 and **7** (★★★★): Kindred spirits, to a great degree. You each possess aspects of character the other one lacks. As the **1**, you can rally your **7** friend out of lethargy or self-pity; and your **7** listens to your problems, without interruption. You also enjoy many of the same things.

1 and **8** (★★★★): If you enjoy a strong introspective tie with your **7** friends, you will thrive on an outdoor/physical friendship with an **8**. You might play tennis or run together, and you are competitive in a healthy way. This friendship grows with passing years.

1 and **9** (★★★★): Another good friendship. These higher numbers balance out your energies and help direct your thoughts. You also have a knack for drawing a **9** friend out of too much personal contemplation or moodiness. **9** is honest with you, which you like.

1 and **11** (★★★): You two often become friends because you attract each other's originality and intelligence – yet it is not without sparks! The chief difficulty is that you tend to tread on each other's toes, or want the same things. This friendship is up and down.

1 and **22** (★★★): Another friend you admire and feel drawn to, but competitiveness and a lack of understanding about the way you each tackle life leads to some problems. You'll get on brilliantly with some **22**s, and not at all with others, depending on other numbers present.

1 IN OTHER PLACES

So what does it mean when your number turns up on a house? Do you live in a 1 home? And how does the number 1 affect your pet – or even the car that you drive? Numbers exude a subtle influence on everything in our lives; and here are just a few examples of how ...

A 1 address

If the number of your address – or of your apartment – reduces back to a **1**, your home will have a distinctiveness about it that makes it stand out from any other in the street or block. It will announce itself as the home of someone different and individual; and it has a personality all of its own, however you choose to decorate it. You will either love its character or totally reject it: that's up to you.

Fascinatingly, a **1** house – even when shared by a couple or a family – often seems to attract owners and occupants who find themselves spending countless hours alone, or feeling isolated while they are in it. This will suit many people perfectly – if you are writing or studying, for instance, or if the home needs to support your quiet time while a partner travels. But, for many, a **1** house can seem to inflict loneliness, and this is something you will need to consider seriously before you move in!

A 1 pet

If you don't know your pet's birthday, use the first letter of their name to calculate their number. If it's an A, J or S, they're a **1**. A **1** pet is an animal you take on and agree to live with by its own rules: for example, the cat who has its own schedule of appearances, who explores the neighbourhood independently – and gets into scrapes you can't always charm your way out of with others! Or, the dog who takes *you* for a walk, bounding off to suit itself, and undecided whether to come when you call, not sure its particularly interested in what's on the menu tonight.

Slightly eccentric, very independent and wonderfully imaginative, this animal will have a delightful sense of humour and seem different to all others of its breed. And would you be attracted to it, if it were any less?

A 1 car

If the numbers of your licence plate reduce to **1**, it's a one-off. Possibly a bold colour, certainly distinctive, and absolutely a character, whether only a piece of metal or not, this car is the property of someone who admires its uniqueness. It seems made for you alone, and asks people to look at both of you.

It won't always behave as you expect, and you may not want to put friends in it for long journeys, as it is choosy about who gets to ride inside. But best, it becomes an extension of your sense of yourself. Oh, and it's probably pretty zippy – or maybe even *really* fast.

YOUR LIFE NUMBER
Your lesson to learn

The time has come to consider the other main number in your numerology chart: your Life Lesson, or LIFE, number. This is sometimes also called the 'Birth Force'. Just as for the DAY number, calculating your LIFE number is easy: simply add together each digit of your full birth date (day, month and year), and keep adding the digits until they reduce to a single number (*see example on page 270*).

And that's it. You have your Life number. So what does it tell us?

What does it mean?

The LIFE number takes times to show its mark. You should see its influence over many years, and understand that it is representative of certain strengths and weaknesses that we learn to live with through years of experience. These characteristics need to be analysed over time, and it can take a while for us to come to know ourselves truly from our LIFE number. Uncovering these aspects of our character is a process of discovery, and we often don't fully recognize the traits of this number as clearly, or as quickly, as those of the stronger DAY number.

Once you have done your sums and discovered this second important number, you'll want to find out what this means. If your LIFE and DAY numbers are the same, this powerfully reinforces the qualities of your own number, and accentuates both strengths and weaknesses. You won't be fighting corners within your personality by having two numbers to live with that are, perhaps, miles apart in spirit. But then, equally, if your numbers are the same you may lack a broad vision of the world, seeing with very sharp eyes through just a single (though enormous!) window.

On the following pages we will examine what your **DAY** number **1** is like in tandem with each other number, beginning with the powerful doubling of **1 DAY** and **1 LIFE**, and then moving on through all other possible combinations. If you discover you have a **LIFE** number which totals **11** or **22**, before it reduces to a final single digit of **2** or **4**, read the entry for **1** and **2**, or **1** and **4**, but also pay special attention to any extra information given relating to the added significance of the number being a variation of a master number.

SAME **DAY** AND **LIFE** NUMBER

With 1 as both of your principal birthday numbers, you must be prepared to forge ahead relentlessly in life, never to lose heart or turn back from your path. It can be a lonely road, and you will be expected time and again to be responsible for yourself. Your friends admire your strength of character and resilience: you pick yourself up and dust yourself off whenever you take a fall. You are a model of independence, but others would be amazed to know you are often racked with fears and self-doubt, although you rarely admit it. You project an image of confidence, and you have a well-honed instinct for what will turn out.

You have great physical stamina, and concentrate your efforts towards an end goal very well. You have excellent agility and good physical timing, and these strengths may aid you in your journey to reach your individual destiny – sometimes in odd ways. It is your task to discover how to inject something fresh and new to the tired old methods you see around you. You always attract audiences prepared to listen to your originality; and you will find several expressions for your talents. This implies a number of possible changes of vocation, or a variety of 'hobby interests', which may eventually become more than a pastime.

You really don't like any kind of restraint, and you expect to be first at whatever you do. This means you will frequently be consulted for ideas at work, or in personal situations, and you will take the lead, bringing executive skills and incisive analysis which can be acted on in any crisis. Some people regard you as a pioneer or, perhaps, an oddball, but the fact remains that you will be followed in every emergency. Eventually you will learn that you work best alone, though it'll be a challenge to try to co-operate with the people around you without compromising your own abilities. While you seldom put yourself in positions which restrict you, you need to accept that you are not automatically right *all* the time. Listen to others too.

Double trouble?

Because **1** is a male number, women carrying this number in double strength are often seen as masculine or aggressive, and two **1**s so prominently placed may well make you brusque or abrasive. It is certainly a physical, active number, and over the years you will become a determined and courageous person. You may be forced to assume authority or leadership without having asked for it, but you will manage – and ultimately thrive – in the role.

A double **1** may be compared by friends and lovers

more with their father than their mother, due to the masculine force of this number. Also, female **1**s are caught between the urge to nurture a family and to compete at the top in a business environment. Somehow, you will find a way through, but it can take half a lifetime to feel you aren't failing at one role because of the other. Female double **1**s usually also have more men friends than women friends, and as much strength as any man. Their 'backbone' is relied upon by all who know them.

Happier mixing with other individuals than in a crowd, you are discerning and disciplined, and yet dynamic in company. You are an activist, with no time for talkers rather than doers. It's true to say most double **1**s are dictatorial without recognizing this, and can be self-obsessed or insensitive towards others' feelings. This is something you must learn to govern. Be selective about the relationships you enter into, and find a partner who understands your impatience to achieve in life – someone who is not averse to playing a supporting role when it is required. Your projects often need careful nursing to fruition, and this will occur more smoothly if your partner is equally self-motivated and confident.

Keep things in check

You don't mean to neglect loved ones, but you do. Just try to find a way of asking for help from your friends when you need it, instead of expecting them to guess. Consider that, although they love you, even your family sometimes see you as a bit of a know-it-all, and lose their patience with you. Your positive qualities are attractive, and will become more pronounced across your life span, but you will have to fight unintentional selfishness or bombastic behaviour if you want to hang on to friends and lovers.

Your perception is extra keen, and you possess a vision for the world, understanding how to get things moving when others have stalled. You also have a delightful humour, and can break the tension in all circumstances. You are enthusiastic, fiery, a person with a strong mind. But the negative qualities of your double number are likely to become more apparent with age, and should be kept under control as much as possible. Don't be too set in your mind, or ignore what someone else is saying; you can appear unintentionally bossy or arrogant, or show little tact for the feelings of others. You may appear to lack humility, or be too preoccupied with your own values, world and wishes. Be alert to this, and make the most of your exceptional audacity and inventiveness.

DIFFERENT **DAY** AND **LIFE** NUMBERS

Most of us will find that we have two different birthday numbers, and this can be an advantage. One number may soften the single track of the other, and mean we can see other people's viewpoints more easily. At other times, though, the numbers may be in real conflict – and this leads to vacillation in our reactions to everyday situations, or confusion about why we want to run one way and then another.

In the following pages you will discover how your own two numbers are likely to work together, and what you can do to maximize the potential of both when they are paired up.

1 Day with 2 Life

Overall, this is a fortuitous blend of a strong and a gentle number. **1** tells us you have good ideas and energies, but you can become dictatorial and dominating sometimes. **2** assuages this, helping you to consult others and intuit their viewpoint. On the other hand, **2** sometimes gets bogged down by too much self-consciousness and attention to negative detail, and **1** can overcome this. **2**'s worst failing – the inclination to dissipate time – is remedied by the boldness of a **1 DAY** number.

Much of your personal sense of style is dictated by your **LIFE** number, and the power and charisma of the **1** balances the shyness of the gentler and more retiring **2**. **1** helps you emit an outward capability and self-sufficiency, but your **2 LIFE** number makes it easy for others to approach you and see you as friendly rather than overawing. Your two numbers are complementary, male and female, and help you project a gentle but positive persona. Your **DAY** number still ensures that you are highly individualistic in your desires, inclinations and fashion sense and taste, but **2** helps you to adjust to circumstances, and understand how to consult other people about what is required. In short, **2** makes you more flexible and offsets some of that **1** aggression.

Both numbers are creative, and the musicality of **2** suggests you might have real talent in this area, because of the **1**'s singularity of mind and its ability to compose or invent. You will have excellent rhythm, and probably be a good dancer, and you also know how to relate well creatively to another individual being. More importantly, you are much more patient than a **1** is generally, and you will take whatever time is required to learn a skill and utilize it. The patience bestowed on you by the number **2** is one of the blessings of having these numbers together, as is the advantage of understanding how to co-operate with others.

If your **2** is actually an **11**, you will have a very good eye for design and line. **1** also loves original creations, so you probably prefer subtle designer clothes and unusual items. You hate to be dressed just like everyone else, but you are ready to put on pastel – or even neutral – colours, with the harmony that comes from these two numbers. Your choice of colour may be daring and, as an **11**, you are more unafraid than any other **2** to draw attention to yourself socially through your choice of style. You marry discretion with flair, and never want to look bland!

The numbers **1** and **11/2** together will sometimes pull you in opposite directions – **1** making you courageous, but **11** very sensitive to nuance, and cautious. If you are mildly eccentric as a result of this disparity, you may choose clothes and interior decoration in your home or office just to shock others, and this sometimes goes deliberately beyond the limits of what a plain **2** would consider tasteful. But you may just carry it off!

1 Day with 3 Life

These two numbers are sometimes at loggerheads when they meet as two individuals, but operating within one personality they usually find much better expression. The effect of **1** and **3** is to heighten the creativity of your **DAY** number and make you very driven to produce artistic perfection. Both numbers are energetic, and the **1**'s single-mindedness dominates the **3**'s distressing indecisiveness: you will get things done! **3** also adds an emotional power, which helps push you to do things that matter even more to your sense of fair play.

Sometimes the **1** pulls the **3 LIFE** number into even greater extravagance than usual, for **1** can show off a little and be impulsive. But a happier outcome is that the **3** adds to **1**'s ambition and dynamism a gift for talking or writing, and a true talent shines out. With the support of your **3 LIFE** number, you will learn over the years how to talk to people, and not to retire into your own shell when you are hurt. **3** adds happiness and optimism to your birthday number, and allows you to mix with a wider group of people than **1** often chooses to do. Equally, the scattered energies one associates with **3** are refined through **1**'s determination, so that the self-expression of both numbers is at a peak.

The one danger of having **1 DAY** and **3 LIFE** numbers joined together is that your excellent ideas get lost in too much talk. **3** is a chatterer, and given to some degree of exaggeration, while **1** likes the sound of its own voice, at times, and can be boastful. If these traits exacerbate each other, there is a wastefulness and a chance of giving in to delusions of grandeur which eclipses the inspirational strengths of both numbers, normally so positive. There is also a possibility that both numbers lapse from genuine innovation to faddishness, and fail to produce anything outstanding. Generally, though, the artistic drive of these two numbers is sufficient to help you work well with your talents and achieve a great deal over your lifetime, and the warm-heartedness of **3** will steer **1** away from its potential to loneliness.

If anyone offends you, you may be especially unforgiving, for **3** hates to have its kind nature thrown in its face. Perceptiveness should help you avoid this, though, and if you are quick to anger you are just as quick to move on. Always make sure there are elements of creativeness in your work or your leisure hours, for without this you may feel as though you have been denied something important in your life.

1 Day with 4 Life

These numbers are likely to act as a brake on one another. It's in **1**'s nature to lead and get on with things, break new ground and throw caution to the wind; and it's in **4**'s nature to do just the opposite. In two different people, these differences normally settle into a dominant/subservient partnership, the **4** adding sobriety when needed. Together in one person's make-up, however, you are likely to find yourself caught between two different standards of what seems acceptable throughout your life. Your **1 DAY** number urges you to be brave and outrageous, while your **4 LIFE** number is conservative and careful. **1** tells you to tear up the rules whenever they seem outmoded, and **4** fits in with society's dictates quite happily. So, which will dominate?

At any given time, either may. Your first inclination – as **1** is the **DAY** number – will be to answer back, walk out when you are cross, or refuse to take 'no' for an answer. On consideration, though, over many days, the practical side of your **4 LIFE** number may urge you to reconsider. Never go off half-cocked, therefore, or you will come to be embarrassed and confused by your own behaviour. And then again, sometimes the self-loathing you may feel about a sense of cowardice that cuts in after an initial adrenaline surge to *do* something may be acute and unhelpful. You will be annoyed with yourself for shrinking away from a fight of any kind.

At best, there is a strong chance that maturity will help you utilize the staying power of the **4** and add it to the initial drive of the **1**, so that after a good idea manifests in your brain you are able to find the persistence to see through what you begin. And, that overly serious side to your character which comes from the **4** will learn to laugh at itself as time goes by – the **1** allowing you to see that some rules and restraints are just silly, and become self-imposed limitations. Try not to let the doubts of **4** creep in and question your creative powers or your imagination.

If the two numbers could help each other, much could be done. This will work out truest when the **4** is actually a **22**, for **22** is the higher-power variant of **4**, and allows much more daring and a broader view of the world altogether. In fact, if you are a **1** and **22/4**, you will be quite an act for anyone to follow! **1** initializes projects, but the **22** would help you carry them to a much higher office. Such a pair of numbers will appear in someone with their own high-power business, or in an actor, perhaps, or someone attracted to politics.

1 Day with 5 Life

Two numbers full of drive, a **1** and **5** working together will push you to over-achieve in life. You are more hot-headed than any other **1** combination, but you have more versatility and charisma too. **1** and **5** are the best numbers for ideas and being quick off the mark, and full of action. Both numbers have a sharp intelligence, and are naturally curious and driven to investigate what is what. Neither likes to sit around waiting for life to knock on the door.

The worst attribute of these numbers together is that impulsiveness and discontent about the way things are is likely to be acute. Also, the **5 LIFE** number gives your **DAY** number a rashness that often erupts as stinging or cruel words directed towards anyone you find slow-witted or dull in temperament. You are critical, and dissatisfied with numerous things, and this can only be remedied if you force yourself not just to dream up improvements and revisions, but actually *implement* them.

You are very physical, probably good at sport, and you enjoy being a spectator of sport, too. The two numbers direct you to travel and see the world, and to expand your work radius as far as you can. You are bound to be appointed as a speaker at whatever you do, and to be a public relations person or a front-of-house executive. And, you may work hard and long, and not mind odd hours – for both the **1** and the **5** drive you to variety, and away from being tied down.

This can be a problem in your private life, though, for the **5** side of your nature wants its freedom, and the **1** also likes its independence. There is obviously space here for things to go wrong, and for misunderstandings to occur with your partners. However, these are energetic and exceptionally creative numbers, and both of them want to cover the canvas that is life with a colourful splash. In other words, you may make mistakes and offend some people, but they'll certainly know you were here!

You have a distinctive style, a particular preference for the modern over the antique when it comes to decoration of your home, and a feel for what will be important in the days to come. **5** is ultra-modern, and helps that innovative **1** imagination to fire on all cylinders. Watch your tendency to over-indulge, though, as the demands and pressures you place yourself under are likely to need release, and over-drinking or overeating can become a problem. You may also be unable to avoid the temptation to have more than one love interest – partly because an unconventional lifestyle puts you in odd places. Consider what may run counter to your eventual happiness.

1 Day with 6 Life

These numbers might discomfit each other, coming together in two different people meeting at a party, but working as the two principal numbers within a single individual they seem to donate richly diverse talents from opposite sides of the numerological 'gene pool', and make a greater whole for it.

As one number is a generous giver and the other an unabashed taker, if these are your two numbers you have the best of both worlds. You will know when to look and when to leap – you have creative patience and the self-discipline to be a good learner and an even better teacher; but you also have the confidence to act on your feelings, and you know how to tackle impossible situations. If **6**'s problem is often to give too much ground to others, or be self-sacrificing to a personally damaging degree, the self-worth that comes with **1** saves you. Equally, the **6**'s inherent sensitivity prevents the abrasive hurtfulness that **1**s usually cause without intending to.

Both numbers are creative, but the **6** is truly artistic, so the pairing of capabilities is very likely to express itself in the arts. Also, study will be a naturally desired pastime, with many people marvelling throughout your lifetime at how much you know in a variety of disciplines. **6** is always gently curious, and **1** has the decisiveness to investigate any situation if it doesn't know the answer. This promotes a good balance for your intellectual focus.

In romantic matters, the **6** softens **1**'s instinct to be alone, and of being unsure how to ask for – or give – love. **6** is the very number of love, and having both numbers makes emotional feelings less of a problem. That said, however, **6** must be loved at all costs, and **1** has impossible standards for a partner to live up to, so you will probably be very choosy before you eventually settle down.

Shared traits between the numbers include artistic and aesthetic appreciation, and a sense of idealism about what can be done in the world ... while on the contradictory side, **6** loves domesticity and has stubborn, slightly conventional opinions, whereas **1** is a freedom-lover and wants to move forwards. Resolving these differences is going to be the interesting bit, and it won't always come smoothly; but it does mean that you will often surprise even yourself in your reactions to emotions, dramas and events. Maturity may make it easier for you to know which way you'll jump in a crisis!

1 Day with 7 Life

This makes you competitive. You are clever, and you know it, but it is never enough to be just 'one of the clever ones'. You need to be at the top of your game all the time, and you will learn from your mistakes well. Your mind is finely disciplined and, though you are sensitive to others' criticisms of you, you are even more critical of yourself. You have a sharp analytical faculty married to a fast tongue, so journalism or writing will have an appeal for you. But heaven help those who annoy or hinder you, because you have a long memory and an utter dislike of fools.

This is a very private number-pairing. You really do need quiet time, and you will brood when feeling stressed or threatened. Circumstances will frequently foist private time upon you, and often you will deliberately push yourself out of your comfort zone just to challenge your mind and energies. Once the world around you becomes a known quantity, you will look to other stimuli to see how you fare, and at times this is both laudable and crazy! Something in you cannot settle, but setting yourself difficult objectives is part of what you're here for. Just don't be surprised if those who share your life become both confused and frustrated by this tendency.

You're not only original, but also a specialist. Nothing irks you more than dilettantism, and you will force yourself through some high hoops to learn everything there is to know about a subject. This makes you a first-class teacher, and many people who have these two numbers will be drawn by academic study and vocation. The solitude of research and writing up your findings will suit you too. On top of this, **1** plus **7** is a bookish number-combination and, whatever genre you prefer, you will read a great deal. You also have a love of art and architecture, and an intellectual interest in metaphysical subjects.

With both of these numbers you may not have a large family, for the emphasis is on the intensity of personal bonds. Love will never be easy, either, for you ask a lot and you want to give particular aspects of yourself. Neither one of these numbers would settle for anything routine or humdrum, nor are they likely to have a conventional lifestyle. Put both together and you double the effect. You will alternately like (and need) both city and countryside, and you will definitely benefit from away-days which take you to the green world, or to the water. A vista of trees or the sea is part of what helps you to think philosophically, and such a sea- or landscape is bound to feature in the life you arrange.

1 Day with 8 Life

Who will succeed at business in this world if you don't? These two numbers understand that, while money isn't everything, without it life is harder. You will almost certainly work for yourself, or independently, and you will work very hard in fits and starts. In fact, you work hard and play hard, and can have extraordinary bursts of physical energy when you need it ... which translates as: watch the inclination to push yourself too hard, at times! And in this life that often seesaws between work and play, family and finance, don't be surprised if you make and lose, and then remake, many fortunes or successful lines of expression. Each of these two numbers can be prone to win, lose and win again, but with both together this kind of oscillation seems unavoidable. Perhaps it is really your way of putting yourself through perpetual challenges?

So bold are your two numbers that you are sure to be in authority, or given authority, throughout life. These numbers are efficient and well-organized, so, taken together, they give you an extra shot of capability and a will that is difficult to appease. You ask a lot of yourself, but you are also very demanding of others, and short of sympathy for those you see as uninspired or lacking in imagination. This can be a problem for you, because the pressure you put on yourself to attain certain high standards in life – and, especially, critical praise for what you do – makes you easy prey for those who don't understand what you are trying to achieve. Others being jealous of you will also be a problem at times, although usually your **DAY/LIFE** combination makes you fairly popular and well-recognized.

Relationships are a strange subject, because you value your freedom and the right to do things your own way. This means you may make things harder for yourself, and women with these two numbers often bypass any partner who could offer them financial security, purely because they don't like to relinquish control of their own affairs. Men with these numbers, on the other hand, may only be excited by a partner who is just as independent and driven as they are – which sets the tone for future competitiveness.

Impatience becomes a greater problem, when **8** is added to your **DAY 1**, so often these two numbers mean that, even in childhood, there is a sense of unstoppable drive to get on with life and do things: there is no time like the present for you, in every way. Don't let this instinct deprive you of fun or relaxation; otherwise, in middle age you could experience premature burn-out, or a loss of any thrill about life. Always remember that this pair of numbers belongs to someone with vision and ambition, and that working towards a cause will usually satisfy your feelings of self-worth.

1 Day with 9 Life

Life has awarded you a very evenly balanced pair of birthday numbers. In a sense, perhaps, nothing could be more desirable than having both a **1** and a **9**, for you can see the start and the end of all things. You have the initial momentum to embark on a plan and the steadiness to see it through, and you show special dramatic flair, which may help kick things off with a bang. You are bound to make a splash in the world.

Your talents are truly diverse, so one problem of this number-pairing is that you often feel torn about which direction to take. You will certainly have big opportunities to show what you're made of, but you can become careless about this, because you expect to do things easily, and to have plenty of invitations in life – both socially and in terms of business propositions. This can cause you to dissipate your chances, and be led to regret that the **1** makes you more arrogant and feisty than might be wise.

To get the best from both numbers, you need to draw on the self-respect you take from your **DAY** number and harness this with the good fellow-feeling you have from **9**. This will make you less likely to offend others, or feel out of touch with their experiences. **9** is so gifted at knowing how another person is inside, whereas **1** is impatient with folly or perceived weakness. Use the charitable and forgiving side of **9** to offset this intolerance.

Your **DAY** number lends you a world view that anything is possible, and you like to achieve things on your own merits. What you borrow from **9** is the degree of perfectionism which allows you to reach really significant milestones, and you will also have exactly what it takes to lead the cavalry charge when it comes to any rescue mission – either of an individual person whom you see as oppressed, or of a social cause that needs a champion. You can give tirelessly, and **9** always helps you to see the bigger picture. Fortunately, those tireless energies that come with your **1** give you hope that you really *can* make a difference, whereas **9** alone is sometimes left feeling so sad about the world and the pain in it.

You will have money in your life, and probably some degree of luck in love. Your **DAY** number, of course, is rather private, and often feels alone and unhelped by anyone, but **9** softens this trait and brings you many friends and admirers. This you usually repay with considerable compassion for others – not always easy for a straight **1** to find!

THE FUTURE

Take a look what's in store...

And now we come to the calculation of your future. Each year, on your birthday, you move into a new sphere of number-influence which governs that year. The numbers progress in cycles of nine years; after nine years, the cycle starts over again, and a whole new period of your life begins afresh. The cycle can be applied to every number, so you can discover what the main issues will be for partners, friends and family, as well as for yourself, in any given year (*see calculation instructions, opposite*). Emphasis is placed on what will happen to you when you are in your own year number – that is, in any '1' year cycle.

Working out your cycle

To find out what year you're currently in, use the same formula employed for calculating the **LIFE** number, but substitute the current year for the year in which you were born. Every year, the cycle then moves on by one more number until, after a **9** year, returning to **1**, to begin the cycle again.

Calculation example 1

BIRTHDAY:	28 May 1966
TO CALCULATE THE CURRENT YEAR NUMBER:	2+8+5+[2+0+0+7 (CURRENT YEAR)] = 24, and 2+4 = **6**

This means that on 28 May 2007 you move into a **6** *year. On 28 May the following year, this would then move into a* **7** *year (2+8+5+2+0+0+8 = 25, and 2+5 =* **7***), and the year after that, an* **8** *year, and so on.*

9 8 7 6 5 4 3 2 1

Calculation example 2

BIRTHDAY: 10 November 1972

TO CALCULATE THE CURRENT YEAR NUMBER: 1+0+1+1+[2+0+0+7 (CURRENT YEAR)] = 12, and 1+2 = **3**

This means that on 10 November 2007 you move into a **3** *year. On 10 November the following year, this would then move into a* **4** *year (1+0+1+1+2+0+0+8 = 13, and 1+3 =* **4***), and the year after that, a* **5** *year, and so on.*

Many numerologists feel that the impact of a year number can be felt from the first day of that year – in other words, from 1st January. However, the usual school of thought is that the new number cycle is initiated *on your birthday itself*, and my experience tends to corroborate this. So, if your birthday is fairly late in the year – November or December, say – this means that you will have gone through most of the calendrical year before *your* new number-year cycle for that year begins.

Look back over some recent years, and see if – in the descriptions on the following pages – you can pinpoint the moment when your yearly number-cycle for any given year became apparent. You'll be amazed at just how accurate this system seems to be.

A 1 year

This is the perfect moment for you, as a **1**, when you can set up new and quite specific long-term goals, and consider just where you want to be a few years from now. You will have different people around you from this point on, and fresh ideas about them and the interests they awaken in you. This is a completely new chapter in your life, and you should set goals for a better and more fulfilling future.

Career-wise, a **1** year often occurs at a time of new employment, or of a complete change in direction in your working life. You are probably wanting to develop new skills or make use of untested talents. You have to believe in yourself now. This is the time when it's a little easier to step back and see how to get started along a particular path. Goals, you will understand, are perfectly attainable, even if a year ago they seemed unrealistic. In a

1 year you have tremendous focus and independence, and excellent determination.

The secret to your success now is in your ability to concentrate; but, emotionally, things can be quite testing. No matter how strong a love bond may be in your life, a **1** year demands that you do much for yourself. You could feel isolated or unsupported, even if someone dear is close by. This is a test of your own courage and inner strength. Only your strongest desires will gain results ... but then, your desires should be fierce during this cycle. Try not to act impulsively, as the push to do so will be powerful, but also, don't be afraid to be independent and go your own way. Strong urges are driving you – forward, for the most part – and no one will thrive in a **1** year better than you!

A 2 year

A year which demands co-operation and partnerships at every level, **2** is a gentle year cycle, when you can consolidate what you started in the previous twelve months. You will need to be diplomatic and sensitive towards other people's feelings, but your intuition is very strong now, and you are able to share the load and the initiative more than you were allowed last year. For this reason, don't try to push things too far or too fast. After the previous whirlwind year, this is a moment to take your time and get things right.

Relationships come more into focus during a **2** year. This is especially pleasing if someone new entered your life in the last year or so, for the vibration of **2** helps a bond to strengthen, and a feeling of mutuality improves now. In some ways you may feel the desire or the need to be secretive, but this is because there are unknown elements at work all on fronts. It will affect you at work and at play, and in a close tie you will discover new tenderness that will probably separate you from other friends. If there is no one special currently in your life, this may be the year to find someone: a **2** year brings a relationship much stronger than a fling!

Your negotiation skills and ability to guess what another person is feeling may work very well for you this year; and, if the number **2** derives from master number **11** (which it almost surely will), there is a chance for serious partnerships and master opportunities. You will need to look at contracts carefully, and spend time on legalities. But this is often the most exciting and unusual year out of the nine. Mysteries come to light, and your ideas flow well. Just be prepared to consider another person in every equation.

A 3 year

Time for you! This twelve-month period is concerned with developing your abilities and testing your flexibility. Your imagination is especially strong, and you may have particular opportunities to improve your wealth and make lasting friendships. You will also need to be focused, because the energy of a **3** year is fast and furious, and may make you feel dissolute. Usually, though, this is a happy year spent with some travel prospects and many creative inspirations. Difficulties which intruded in the previous two years are often resolved in this year cycle.

Business and your social life often run together in a **3** year, and work will be a lot of fun. It is worth taking time over your appearance and indulging yourself more than usual, for the sociability of this number brings you many invitations and a chance to create a new look, or to explore other aspects of your personality. You have extra charm this year, so try to use it where it is needed.

Many people find that the number **3** expresses itself in a year cycle as a third person to consider: frequently, this is the birth of a child or an addition to the family, but it might be that another party pressures you in your personal relationship. Don't talk too much about this, or show nervousness. Under a **3** vibration, it is easy to become exhausted – even through over-excitement – so be alert to the impulse towards extravagance and fragmentation. Try to enjoy the way in which you are being drawn out of yourself this year, and allow yourself time to study, write, paint. Anything you really want you can achieve now – even strange wishes and desires can be pulled towards you. Make sure you think a little about what you are asking for!

A 4 year

A much-needed year of good-housekeeping – on the personal level, as well as literally. This year will demand practicality from you. Often a **4** brings a focus on money or accounts, on repairs around the home, or on putting your life into better order. It may not be what you want, yet it will force itself upon you. It is sometimes a year spent with a pen in hand – writing lists or cheques, doing sums and keeping diaries. It is also a year when you will need to do some research, to find out about what you don't know.

You have so much work to do in a **4**, or **22**, year – more than for a long time. Your personal pleasure takes second place to requirement, and it may seem difficult to stick to the task sometimes. Money demands that you do so, for extra expenditure is not advised in this twelve-month period. Yet if this sounds stressful, it also gives you a feeling of satisfaction that you will achieve so much this year – a job of hard work and dedication really well done. It may be that this year gives you a very good foundation for the future and sets up lasting improvements.

You will never survive a **4** – or, especially, a **22** – year if you are not organized and implement a system of work and life. Be honest in what you do with others, but also in what you do for yourself. You cannot deceive yourself, and must check details carefully. You may have a feeling of burden at times, but there is a chance to feel you have done something extraordinary too. Translate your clever ideas into practical results. The most significant thing for you to do is to concentrate on proper personal management. The weight of the world is on your shoulders, but you can bear it if the preparations you make are good. There is no escape from demands on your time and intelligence, but nothing can be hurried, so face the job ahead and you will soon find you have climbed a hill to new vistas.

A 5 year

After careful management of your time last year, and a feeling of being tied to the wheel, this will seem like bursting from the inside of a darkened room into bright light. Now you have a change from routine to madness, and you may feel a personal freedom that was denied you last year. Nevertheless, nothing is completely settled in a **5** year, and this uncertainty may take its toll. Try to look at this cycle as a chance to find success in newer areas, and a way to advance from necessary stagnation into running waters of energy and vitality. You will update your sense of yourself during this period, and make progress towards the life you want, following the previous year's required self-discipline.

You are admitting to the need for new pastures, so your ideas of what your life might include, or who may have a role in it, may alter now. No one likes to be held back in a **5** year, but it is still important not to be too hasty in your actions. Use your energies, by all means, but govern them with your head. This is the time for innovation, and new takes on old goals, but if you quarrel with those dear to you, or with whom you work, it may be difficult to repair later. If change is still inevitable, be as kind and constructive as possible, and make sure you aren't leaping from one difficult situation straight into another. You need to discover your versatility and personal resourcefulness to get the best out of this cycle. And, for some of the twelve months, travel or lots of movement seems inescapable.

This year is potentially some kind of turning point for you. Learning how to adapt to sudden circumstances is vital, because any plans or directives set in stone will cause you pain, and possibly come unstuck. Be prepared for changes and, if this brings a nervousness with it, try to meet the adventure head-on. If you talk yourself up and take on a front-running position, you can work wonders in a **5** year.

A 6 year

Love is in the air. Other things seize your time too – your home needs attention, and duties demand your energy – but, principally, this year is about emotions and relationships. Sometimes love and happiness are a reward for surviving so much in the past two years, and for unselfish service and support for others. The emphasis is on finding harmony with others, and this may come in various ways. This year, you may have the impetus and opportunity to erase problems that have previously beset you. You understand, and feel acutely sensitive towards, others, and are more radiant and beautiful than you have been for some time. If you can be kind and positive in emotional dealings, you will benefit in many ways, including materially.

There are hurdles in a **6** year in connection with obligations you feel towards others. At times you are stretched, because there are personal desires and ties you want to nurture which are countermanded by the duties you are subjected to. You may resent this, yet, if you can remain cheerful, you will be rewarded in ways not immediately apparent. Love is trying to sweep you off your feet, but your health may suffer because you are trying to fit in so much, and the intensity of your feelings is strong.

While it's good to be helpful in a **6** year, don't allow yourself to be taken advantage of, or let people drain you completely. Set up a system that lets you delegate some responsibility. Your home may bloom while you're in such a happy mood, and you should feel creative and mellow. The events of a **6** year are not as fast and furious as the previous year, but things move steadily towards a happier state of being. Let the time go as it will, because this is not a year to fight against what comes to you; get into the right philosophical gear and open yourself to pleasant surprises that come from being useful, and being warm with others.

A 7 year

This year is a time for manifesting your goals by visualizing them. See yourself triumphing and continuing toward your vision. Never lose sight of what you want, or confusion will reign. You'll be tempted this way and that, annoyed by gossip, and attacked by those who love you but don't understand what you are trying to do. Don't be swayed by them, or you will lose your opportunities and precious time.

Keep your head, as everything depends on your state of mind. Refuse to react to distractions, and avoid hasty actions or sudden decisions. A calm approach is the best remedy to the chaos surrounding you. You may have to move house without warning, but take it in your stride and make a calm, clear choice on where to go. If you are travelling somewhere exotic, be prepared with vitamins and medicines to avoid viruses of any kind.

Legal matters may arise during this year, relating to business, investments or house options. Consult an expert to avoid pitfalls, and, when you feel happy, proceed with confidence. If you have taken all the facts and details into account, you'll now be within sight of your goal. But watch your health, as the number **7** is connected with this subject for both good and ill. You might get fit and lose some weight or, conversely, suffer with some little grievance. This is a time for mental, spiritual and physical detoxing. Also, rest: take a vacation to the country, to a quiet location where you can think in peace. Let no one confuse you. You may have to wait, but you will know how to come out on top if you listen to your intuition.

This is an excellent year for study, research, writing and reading, and clearing out all the unnecessary people or ideas from your past.

An 8 year

This cycle brings the possible finding of a soulmate. If you're single, you could not have a better chance of meeting that special someone than now. **8** years also relate to money, so you may be caught up with an impossible workload and regard the arrival of such a potentially strong love as poor timing – and perhaps this is why it comes to you, because your attention being taken up elsewhere may be the best reason for someone's admiration. The love vibration you experience under karmic year number **8** may point to a future relationship prospect which has a lasting importance.

For those in settled relationships, pregnancy sometimes comes with this number, and it brings a very special link between the child and their parents. Or, you may experience a deep urge to study a subject that comes easily to you, though you have never learned about it before – a language, perhaps, or an artistic skill you were attracted to but never developed, but which you now pick up well. Even a professional subject that you seem to grasp quickly will seem more important to perfect than ever before. Partly, this is because **8** year cycles concern making more money, and dealing with the deeply felt past. There are huge opportunities for you in an **8** year, and you will want to be prepared to maximize them. However, you'll need to use good judgement and be efficient with your time management.

Many people feel pushed to the limit in an **8** year, because there is just so much going on. Consider, though, that the vibration of the number wants to find positive expression, so the more efficiency and determination you can bring to it, the better the chance of finishing on a high note. Don't over-commit your time or money, and be ready to acquiesce to others' ways of doing things. You need to be confident, but ready to adjust too. **8** is made up of two circles, asking 'infinity' of you. But this year, you can do it!

A 9 year

Your personal affairs all come to a head in a **9** year, and whatever has been insufficient, or unsatisfying, will rise to the surface and demand change now. It could be the fulfilment of many dreams, for this is the culmination of nine years' experience. Whatever is jettisoned was probably no longer of use – though this might seem dispassionate. Many friendships will drift away, but you have probably outgrown them. The strongest demand of you is a readiness to discard what will not be part of your serious future – and this can mean a temporary feeling of insecurity.

You will certainly travel in a **9** year. Even if a trip is short, or of no great distance, it will settle something in your mind. The more compassionate, tolerant and forgiving you are, the more warmth and generosity will come to you. This is not the right moment to start something completely new, but if events arise as a natural conclusion to what has gone before, this is a good thing. Your mind needs to engage with bigger issues, for selfishness or petty ideas will cause you unhappiness under this number. People will thwart you in your career and personal matters – and these obstacles seem to come out of the blue, and are beyond your control. However, if you think on philosophical issues and remain open to big ideas, everything will turn out well.

A **9** year can be populated with many friends and activities, yet can feel lonely too; this is a cycle for completion of tasks and the ending of what is not enduring. But this is the right time to see the fruits of your previous work. Be wise about where your destiny seems to want to take you. Your artistic and imaginative facilities are inspired now, and you'll begin to see new directions that you know you must investigate in the years ahead. You know what is missing in your life, or where you've failed yourself, and can now prepare for the new adventure that's about to dawn.

How to find your DAY NUMBER

Add the digits for the day of birth, and keep adding them until they reduce to one number:

EXAMPLES

28 May 1966	2+8 = 10, and 1+0 = **1**
10 November 1972	1+0 = **1**

How to find your LIFE NUMBER

Add the digits for the day, month and year of birth, and keep adding them until they reduce to one number:

EXAMPLES

28 May 1966	2+8+5+1+9+6+6 = 37 3+7 = 10, and 1+0 = **1**
10 November 1972	1+0+1+1+1+9+7+2 = 22 (a 'master' number), and 2+2 = **4**

Further reading

The Complete Book of Numerology, David A. Phillips, Hay House, 2006
The Day You Were Born: A Journey to Wholeness Through Astrology and Numerology, Linda Joyce, Citadel Press, 2003
Many Things on Numerology, Juno Jordan, De Vorss Books, 1981
Numerology, Hans Decoz and Tom Monte, Perigee Books, 2001
Numerology: The Romance in Your Name, Juno Jordan, De Vorss Books, 1977
Sacred Number, Miranda Lundy, Wooden Books, 2006
The Secret Science of Numerology: The Hidden Meaning of Numbers and Letters, Shirley Blackwell Lawrence, New Page Books, 2001

About the author

Titania Hardie is Britain's favourite 'Good Witch' and a best-selling author. Born in Sydney, Australia, Titania has a degree in English and Psychology, and also trained in parapsychology and horary astrology. With a high media profile, she regularly appears on television in the UK, US, Canada, Australia and South Africa, as well as receiving widespread newspaper and magazine coverage. Her previous titles have sold over a million copies worldwide, and include *Titania's Crystal Ball*, *Aroma Magic*, and *Hocus Pocus*. Her first novel is due to be published in summer 2007.

Acknowledgements

Many thanks to you, Nick, for the clear and brilliant vision; you knew what you wanted and, like a true and inspired **1**, kept mulling it over until a way was found. This is your baby. Also big thanks to Tessa, master number **22**, for your commitment to this magnum opus beyond call: only you and I know, Tessa, how much time and soul has gone into all of these words. To Ian, for keeping us piping along with a true **4**'s sanguine approach to such a long body of work, and to Elaine and Malcolm for the look – **6**s, naturally! For my daughter Samantha, thanks for some of your ideas which found expression in the second-to-last section: I love the latte in Soho while signing the author. Let's see! To Georgia, for work in the field on number **5**, my thanks. To all of you, my appreciation, and I wish you all LUCKY NUMBERS!

EDDISON•SADD EDITIONS

Editorial Director **Ian Jackson**
Managing Editor **Tessa Monina**
Proofreader **Nikky Twyman**
Art Director **Elaine Partington**
Mac Designer **Malcolm Smythe**
Production **Sarah Rooney**